Tucson Reflections

Living History from the Old Pueblo

Bob Ring

Book design: Bob Ring

Cover design: Bob Ring

Printed by: Three Knolls Publishing & Printing

International Standard Book Number: 978-1-941138-72-4

Dedication

This book is dedicated to the continuing fight against cancer, a disease that has affected me since 1985.

Cancer has touched my Life

Ann Ring, my beloved wife, and mother of my three incredible sons, was diagnosed with breast cancer in 1985 and after a brave struggle, finally succumbed to the disease in 1990.

Eleven years later in 2001, I met my wonderful second life partner, Pat Wood, who has twice survived breast cancer - experiencing surgery, radiation, and chemotherapy - and has been cancer-free since 2004.

Finally, in 2013/2014 I had three early skin cancers surgically removed from my head - a squamous cell, early melanoma, and basil cell - an experience that my dermatologist referred to as a rare "trifecta."

My objectives with this book

As my small part in battling cancer, I am self-publishing this book and then giving the books away to anyone interested while copies last.

I strongly encourage readers to make a generous donation to an appropriate Tucson cancer treatment or support organization so that we can permanently eradicate this disease and/or ease the burden of those afflicted.

Contents

Introduction

Tucson Reflections - Living History from the Old Pueblo collects, integrates, and updates 29 of my Tucson-history-related newspaper columns [Ring's Reflections] published in Tucson's *Arizona Daily Star* between April 2009 and February 2014. Columns that ran originally as a multi-part series have been combined. Corrections have been made where warranted and selected columns updated with additional information.

The scope of this book includes the major events on the timeline below and several special interest topics.

After a brief but comprehensive Tucson history overview - from prehistoric times to the present, *Tucson Reflections* focuses on the people who helped Tucson develop and who made the important difference: the Old Pueblo's early territorial pioneers and later, after Arizona statehood in 1912, the city's movers and shakers. A presentation of stagecoach history highlights how early overland service through Tucson put the burgeoning town on the U.S. map, followed by a half century of Tucson-centered stagecoach service that enabled hugely important mining development in southern Arizona. Next, the book highlights two historic communities that owed their existence to then plentiful water in Tucson's Rillito River. This is followed by a whimsical, time-travel inspired review of Tucson's growth to the northeast and the development of two of Tucson's more affluent communities. Next, the book addresses Tucson's historic critical resources of mountain riches and life-giving water and finally, spotlights the unique histories of three Tucson buildings.

Tucson Reflections is directed at both Tucson residents and visitors, who hopefully will find "a fresh and vivid look at the history of the area."

Tucson History Timeline.

9,000 BC	Hunter-gatherers reach Tucson from north.
2,000 BC	Farming begins along Tucson's rivers.
AD 450 – AD 1450	Hohokam Culture flourishes in Tucson Valley.
1694	Father Eusebio Kino visits Tucson, expands mission-building in southern Arizona.
1775	Hugo O'Conor establishes Spanish Presidio at Tucson.
1821	Mexico achieves independence from Spain; Tucson belongs to Mexico.
1854	Gadsden Purchase from Mexico makes Tucson part of U.S. territory with New Mexico.
1862	Tucson briefly becomes part of the Confederate States of America during the Civil War.
1863	Abraham Lincoln makes Arizona a separate U.S. territory.
1866-1877	Tucson is first capital of Arizona Territory.
1880	First Southern Pacific Railroad train arrives from west; transcontinental route completed in 1881.
1885	Territorial legislature authorizes the University of Arizona.
1912	President William Howard Taft makes Arizona 48th state of U.S.
1920	Census shows Phoenix replaces Tucson as Arizona's largest city.
1920s	Tucson becomes known popularly as the "Old Pueblo."
1950s	Tucson experiences post World War II industrial growth and population explosion.
1992	Central Arizona Project begins supplying Tucson with water from Colorado River.
2000s	University of Arizona leads advanced technology revolution in Tucson.
2010	Census shows Tucson's metropolitan population exceeds 520,000.

Chapter 1

A Brief History of Tucson

Tucson's First Residents: Hunter Gatherers to Farmers
9,000 BC to AD 450

The first Tucsonans were probably descendants of people who followed herds of large game animals from Siberia across a land bridge in the Bering Strait into Alaska between about 45,000 BC and 12,000 BC. Subsequent generations of these Paleo-Indians (ancient ones) gradually spread southward to populate the Americas. (Note: There are alternative migration starting points, routes, and dates currently under intense study.)

Estimates are that by about 9,000 BC, small bands of hunters had reached the Tucson Valley. The post Ice Age climate was cooler and wetter than today's dry Sonoran Desert. Grasslands thrived. The Santa Cruz River, along with the Rillito River, Pantano Creek, and Tanque Verde Creek, flowed year round. The mountains surrounding Tucson had forests of juniper and pine that extended much farther down their slopes than these trees do today.

Hunter-Gatherers

Populating this landscape were huge mammoths (up to 13 feet high at the shoulders), large bison, giant beavers, grizzly bears, camels, deer, elk, and horses. Besides hunting these animals, the first Tucsonans probably also hunted smaller game and gathered plant food.

Eleven thousand years ago Wooly Mammoths roamed the Tucson area. (From Tucson's International Wildlife Museum, courtesy of Bob Ring)

No skeletal evidence of these early hunter-gatherers has yet been found and they left few traces of habitation. Only a single campsite is known in southeastern Arizona - near Sierra Vista. They ranged over large areas, lived in small groups of 25-30 people, and didn't stay long in one location. Their movements were probably determined by the amount of game, the season, and availability of native plants.

Hunters trapped mammoths and other large animals along streams and lakes and killed them with spears tipped with large razor-sharp, distinctively grooved spear points, called Clovis points, after Clovis New Mexico, a center for this Paleo-Indian Clovis culture.

Five deeply buried kill sites, along with Clovis points and other stone tools, have been found among the bones of mammoths and bison in the San Pedro Valley to the east. Archaeologists have yet to find a kill site in Tucson, but have found two Clovis spear points, one along the Santa Cruz River in the southern Tucson Valley and another in the northern Tucson Valley.

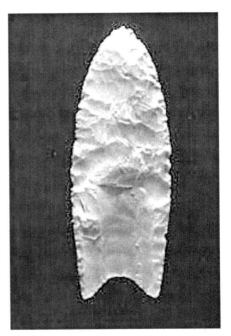

Early Tucson residents hunted mammoths with spears tipped with Clovis points like this one, chipped out of stone. (Courtesy Wikimedia Commons)

As the effects of the last Ice Age receded, the southern Arizona climate continued to warm and dry. Mammoths and other big game animals began to die off, probably because they couldn't adjust to the climate changes, but perhaps because they were killed off by their human hunters. By about 7,500 BC the large mammals were mostly gone.

Desert Culture

People of the Tucson Valley now hunted smaller game such as rabbits, deer, birds, and bighorn sheep at higher altitudes. They stayed in one place longer than their predecessors, supplementing their diet with berries, seeds, nuts, and grains. They maintained seasonal migratory patterns but returned to the same place. They lived primarily in the open, but probably built temporary shelters.

The beginning of this Desert Culture is marked by the appearance for the first time of seed-milling equipment in the form of hand-held stone grinding slabs. Porridge and bread were now a part of the diet.

The only habitation site from this period identified so far in the Tucson Valley was found in what is now known as Dove Mountain in the southern Tortolita Mountains.

By about 3,000 BC the desert people's grinding equipment had evolved to deep basin bottom-stones or mutates, small round handstones or manos, mortars, and large stone pestles. Tucson area sites from this period have been discovered in the Catalina foothills, the Rincon and Santa Rita Mountains, the lower hills of the Tucson Mountains, and alongside the Santa Cruz River and its tributaries.

The Tucson area climate had stabilized by about 2,500 BC, closely resembling the Sonoran desert climate of today.

Farming Begins

In about 2,000 BC corn was introduced to the Tucson Valley from Mexico. Agriculture was an important step to people who had previously relied only on hunting and gathering. The desert people planted corn near camps with permanent water supplies. After planting they resumed hunting and gathering native plant foods, returning to harvest the ripened crop.

By 1,500 BC these early farmers were constructing short irrigation canals along the Santa Cruz River. Flood farming during the summer monsoon season was practiced along the banks of the river and its tributaries by at least 800 BC.

Small farming camps had grown into small agricultural settlements by 400 BC. Such sites have been found in the Tucson Valley on low terraces overlooking the floodplains of Tucson's waterways or buried deeply in floodplain sediments. One such settlement was partially excavated on the site of Tucson's first mission, the historic San Agustin Mission, just east of A-Mountain. Plant remains recovered from these settlements reveal that the farmers grew maize and eventually beans, squash, cotton, and agave.

Excavation of some of these sites has revealed small round or oval pit houses, bell-shaped storage pits, roasting pits, small fire pits, carbonized fragments of corn, and human burials. Other artifacts from this period include marine shell beads and small pendants. Small fire-hardened clay human figures and beads have also been found.

Fired figurines, shell jewelry, bell-shaped pits, and corn farming all developed in Mexico centuries earlier than in Arizona. Marine shells and some of the other materials used in tools and ornaments were not locally available in the Tucson area, suggesting that early Tucson farmers traded with Mexico. Thus began the long-term influence that Mexico would have on Tucson.

By AD 100, undecorated, unpolished pottery (brownware) was widely used in the Tucson Valley as containers or for storage. Reliance on crops continued to increase. Populations grew. Trade in shells, turquoise, and obsidian increased along newly developing trade networks.

The next 350 years saw a long developmental sequence that resulted in increasing the scale of the desert farmers' society. By AD 450 people started coming together in more permanent settlements, built more substantial buildings and massive irrigation systems, and formalized their games and rituals.

As Arizona's well known historian Marshall Trimble puts it, "These desert people were the link between the ancient elephant hunters and prehistoric Hohokam."

The Hohokam and Descendants
AD 450 to AD 1694

In the last 40 years archaeologists have changed their minds about the origin of the prehistoric Hohokam - who built extensive irrigation systems, ball courts, and platform mounds, made beautiful pottery and jewelry, and engaged in wide-ranging trade – and whose culture lasted a thousand years.

The old story - based on a handful of Hohokam site excavations - talked about the Hohokam migrating from Mexico with their distinctive culture already fully developed to settle in villages along the Salt and Gila Rivers near Phoenix in about 300 BC, with a small group moving south to Tucson around AD 200 to live along the Santa Cruz and Rillito Rivers.

The Hohokam Millennium

But today's theory, based on extensive new excavations, summarized by Henry D. Wallace of Desert Archaeology, Inc. in *The Hohokam Millennium*, is that Hohokam culture slowly "developed in place" from relatively short-lived small farming villages of the desert people in the Tucson Valley and then expanded northward to accelerate "the development of permanently settled life … and the emergence of the Hohokam cultural core in the Phoenix area" in about 450 AD.

That is not to say that Mexico did not strongly influence the Hohokam. Scholars now believe that many aspects of Hohokam culture sprang from western Mexico, noting similarities in architecture, pottery, figurines, rituals, religious beliefs, and other artifacts. In turn, western Mexico was influenced by the earlier advanced civilizations in central Mexico and Guatemala, including the Olmecs, Aztecs, and Mayas. Western Mexico then served as a "pass-through" to the Hohokam for certain aspects of art, architecture, and artifacts from these great cultures.

Trade would keep the Hohokam in continual contact with Mexico.

From the huge area of arable land at the junction of the Salt and Gila Rivers, the Hohokam soon expanded over an area in Arizona larger than the state of South Carolina - bounded by the Agua Fria and Verde Rivers to the north, the Mogollon Rim to the northeast, the Dragoon Mountains to the southeast, the Mexican border to the south, and the Growler Mountains to the west.

In the Tucson Valley in AD 450, small Hohokam villages with pit house homes (dug into the ground and covered with brush and dirt) were spread out along the Santa Cruz and Rillito Rivers where the Hohokam could conduct irrigation farming.

Beginning about AD 750 these small river villages grew and seasonal camps in outlying areas were established for hunting and gathering, or limited farming. A number of these riverside villages contained large, basin-shaped ball courts, with earthen embankments, that probably served as sports arenas as well as places to hold religious ceremonies, and other communal activities.

Between AD 950 and 1150, Hohokam settlements dispersed further to farm on fertile areas of Tucson's lower mountain slopes. The population increased and there were more permanent habitations. The largest villages were on terraces just above the Santa Cruz River - with well-built pit houses surrounding central plazas.

This reconstruction of a portion of Hohokam Honey Bee village in Oro Valley shows the village as it might have appeared around AD 1125. (Rob Ciaccio, courtesy Desert Archaeology, Inc.)

Some villages produced decorated red-on-brown pottery for their own use or trade. The Hohokam also made plaited baskets by weaving yucca, cattail, and beargrass into various shapes.

Farming was the Hohokam's main enterprise. Crops included corn, squash, beans and cotton. Cotton was used for both food (in the form cotton-seed cakes) and clothing (where cotton fiber was spun into yarn and woven into ponchos, shirts, and belts).

As opposed to the huge net of irrigation canals (totaling 100s of miles) along the Salt and Gila Rivers to the north, Hohokam in the Tucson Valley built smaller-scale canals and used floodwaters from the Santa Cruz and Rillito Rivers to water their crops.

By AD 1275-1300, most of the smaller villages had been abandoned and settlements in the Tucson Valley had aggregated at only a half-dozen large communities of up to perhaps 2,000 people. Above-ground adobe architecture appeared for the first time. Although corn was still the primary agricultural crop, large rock-pile fields, associated with cultivation of agave (for food and fiber) have been found in both the northern and southern portions of the Tucson Valley.

Platform mounds (elevated platforms supported by dirt fill) were also constructed at a number of Tucson Valley villages in this period. Archaeologists agree that the Hohokam used these mounds for religious ceremonies and rituals, but perhaps also for trade, irrigation control, food and goods dispersal, or social activities. Most importantly, people lived in structures atop the mounds, suggesting an elevated status and the beginning of a social hierarchy.

This illustration of a Hohokam tower-type mound called Pyramid Point in the Tonto Basin shows how it might have looked around AD 1275. (Ziba Ghassemi, courtesy Desert Archaeology, Inc.)

The Hohokam culture was productive and successful without a managing bureaucracy. They had no written language or state-level government.

Remains of major Hohokam villages have been found along the Santa Cruz River at places now occupied by Marana, downtown Tucson, and southern Tucson - and along the Rillito River at Fort Lowell.

By AD 1450 the Hohokam culture had largely disappeared, leaving very little archeological evidence for what happened. Scholars speculate that extended 13th-century draughts, disastrous 14th-century floods, or political instability could have been contributing factors. Others think that deadly new diseases, introduced into central Mexico by Spanish conquistadors in the early 1500s, spread rapidly along trade routes to deal a final devastating blow to the Hohokam.

Descendants of the Hohokam?

There is no clear transition between the Hohokam culture and the people who greeted Italian-born Spanish Jesuit missionary Father Eusebio Kino who first visited south-central Arizona in the early 1690s.

The Papago (now called Tohono O'odham) or "Desert People," lived in the desert, west of Tucson. The Pima (now called Akimel O'odham) or "River People," lived along the Salt, Gila, and Santa Cruz Rivers. A group of Piman natives called Sobaipuris lived in the valleys of the San Pedro and Santa Cruz Rivers. These Native American groups had similar languages and believed in a common origin, according to shared oral traditions.

All of the native groups farmed and foraged for food when crops were poor. They used precious desert water and the rivers to irrigate their crops and successfully raised corn, beans, calabashes, melons, and cotton.

In AD 1694, while traveling northward through the Santa Cruz Valley, Father Kino found a Sopaipuri village called *Schookson* (later called Tucson by the Spanish) - on the west side of the Santa Cruz River at the foot of A-Mountain.

Tucson's age of Spanish missionaries had begun.

Spanish Missionaries
1694 to 1775

By the early 1690s, Spanish colonial policy had been in operation in Mexico for almost 175 years, with Spanish control and influence steadily expanding northward from central Mexico. According to historian Henry F. Dobins in *Spanish Colonial Tucson*, "Colonial officials relied heavily on missionaries to concentrate scattered native populations at a relatively few mission sites" to foster farming and stock-raising, while preparing natives to "become tribute-paying subjects of the Crown." The missionary effort in northern Mexico and southern Arizona was assigned to the Roman Catholic religious order, the Society of Jesus, or Jesuits.

Jesuits

Destined to play a key role in southern Arizona, in lands formerly occupied by the Hohokam, Jesuit missionary Father Eusebio Kino became the first European to explore the Santa Cruz Valley.

In 1692 when Father Kino first visited the Sabaipuri village of *Bac*, about seven miles south of Tucson, he found over 800 natives farming irrigated fields.

When he traveled further north in 1694, Kino reached *Schookson* for the first time and three years later on another visit, he counted 750 people living there in 186 houses stretched out along the river.

At *Schookson*, Father Kino saw that from a combination of the free-flowing river, tapping underground flows in river marshes, plus natural

Father Eusebio Kino was commemorated in this statue by Julian Martinez, located at the intersection of 15th Street and Kino Avenue. (Courtesy of Bob Ring)

springs in the marshes, the natives irrigated their crops using canals probably left behind by the Hohokam. Between A-Mountain and the Rillito River, on the east bank of the Santa Cruz River, the Sopaipuris also irrigated crops in the floodplain. They probably grew corn, beans, squash, melons, and cotton.

Father Kino established more than 20 missions in Mexican Sonora and south-central Arizona, earning the respect of the natives, his fellow missionaries, and his superiors. He founded Mission San Xavier del Bac in 1692 as the northern-most Jesuit mission in southern Arizona.

Between 1694 and his death in 1711, Kino rarely visited Tucson. Other priests from San Xavier and missions farther south occasionally visited Tucson, but with little effect on the religious conversion of the natives.

But, in the words of anthropologist Thomas E. Sheridan, other "events … truly revolutionized human society in Arizona." Father Kino introduced wheat, cattle, horses and mules to the natives along the Santa Cruz River. Other Jesuit missionaries introduced barley, peaches and sheep to complement the native summer crops and wild food resources. The seeds for better agriculture and ranching had been planted.

According to anthropologist Sheridan, "the most important impetus to Spanish settlement" was a silver strike in 1736 in northern Mexican Sonora that resulted in a large migration of Spanish fortune seekers into south-central Arizona. In addition to mining, some of these adventurers were impressed by the fertile Santa Cruz Valley and stayed to farm or start cattle ranches. This brought the interlopers into land conflicts with native Pimas who were already chaffing at perceived harsh treatment by Jesuit missionaries.

In 1751 the Pimas revolted against Spanish control across northern Sonora and south-central Arizona, affecting natives as far north as San Xavier del Bac. Following the deaths of two Spanish missionaries, and over a hundred settlers and peaceful natives, the Spanish military defeated a large force of Native Americans and peace was negotiated.

The next year in 1752, the Spanish set up a fort, or presidio, at Tubac to protect Spanish interests in the Santa Cruz Valley. This was the first permanent Spanish settlement in Arizona.

The first attempt at establishing a permanent mission in Tucson occurred in 1757 when German-born Jesuit Bernhard Middendorff arrived, accompanied by ten soldiers to provide security. But after only five months, Middendorff was driven out by the natives and he fled to Mission San Xavier del Bac, with Tucson reverting to the status of a "branch" mission.

Meanwhile a new force had moved into southern Arizona from the Great Plains, a force that would have a far ranging impact on Spanish colonialism and Tucson. Since the late 1600s, fierce, warlike Apaches had been harassing the Spanish and more peaceful Native Americans, including the eastern Sobaipuris living along the San Pedro River.

With the Sobaipuris much reduced in numbers, in 1762 Spanish Colonial officials, trying to strengthen their northern frontier, ordered Spanish troops to relocate the Sobaipuris from their native land to existing missions to the west. About 250 Sobaipuri came to Tucson. One unfortunate result of this move was the removal of a barrier to Apache plundering to the south and west.

Then suddenly in 1767, King Charles III of Spain expelled the Jesuits from the Americas because their model of independent mission communities didn't fit Spain's emerging desire to exploit their colonial lands and native labor for private gain. For Tucson, nearly 70 years of sporadic Jesuit missionary visits had not had much effect on the natives.

Franciscans

King Charles ordered another Catholic religious order, the Franciscan College of the Holy Cross, to operate the northern Sonora and south-central Arizona missions. The Franciscans assigned Spanish-born friar, Fray Francisco Garcés, to the San Xavier del Bac Mission and the associated natives at Tucson. Immediately after arriving in 1768, Fray

Garcés began splitting his time between *Bac* and Tucson, for the first time providing a continuing religious presence for the natives in Tucson.

After the native village of *Bac* suffered three attacks by Apaches in 1768 and 1769, the military commander at the Spanish presidio in Tubac, Capt. Juan Bautista de Anza, ordered that Tucson natives build a protective wall for their village. Under military supervision, the native Tucsonans completed an adobe structure with towers in early 1771 and later that year a church. This was the first European-style construction at Tucson.

Fray Garcés dedicated the new church to Saint Augustine, thus christening Mission San Agustin del Tucson.

In 1772 Spanish officials began thinking about building new presidios and relocating others to provide a "unified line of defense" against British and Russian interests in the northwest. Spanish soldier, Irish mercenary, Colonel Hugo O'Conor was given the responsibility of selecting the sites.

On August 20, 1775, O'Conor announced his decision to move the presidio at Tubac to Tucson. He apparently recognized Tucson's advantages of established missions at *Bac* and Tucson; ample water, pastures, and wood; and the Native American population, rich fields,

This statue of Tucson founder, Irishman Hugo O'Conor, by Sierra Vista sculptor Brian Donahue, stands in front of the historic Manning House in downtown Tucson. (Courtesy of Wikimedia Commons)

and orchards. The site for the new presidio was to be on the east terrace of the Santa Cruz River, opposite the Native American village and Mission San Agustin del Tucson.

Just after O'Conor made his decision, Juan Batista de Anza, accompanied by Fray Garcés and many of the troops from the Tubac presidio, departed on an expedition to California, where Anza established the first Spanish colony at San Francisco. Short of manpower, the construction of the presidio in Tucson proceeded slowly.

When the California expedition returned in late 1776, having pioneered the future road west along the Gila River, the troops moved into the incomplete new presidio at Tucson.

Thus, at the same time that America was proclaiming its independence from England, 2300 miles to the east in Philadelphia, Tucson was reborn as a Spanish settlement.

Garcés continued his ministry at *Bac* and Tucson through 1779, before moving on to other missions on the Spanish colonial frontier. In 1881 he was killed along the Colorado River by Yuma Indians rebelling against harsh Spanish treatment.

The Spanish/Mexican Presidio
1775 to 1854

Hugo O'Conor became the father of Tucson on August 20, 1775 when, with the authority from Spanish officials, he decided to move the presidio at Tubac to Tucson. Because of a lack of manpower, the fort was not finished until May 1783, completed after revitalized efforts following a disastrous attack by Apache raiders in May 1782.

Spanish Period

The presidio was located where downtown Tucson is today, bounded approximately by Pennington Street on the south, Church Avenue on the east, Washington Street on the north, and Main Avenue on the west. The adobe walls were three feet thick at the base and ten to twelve feet high, along a huge square about 700 feet on a side. There were square towers at the northeast and southwest corners, a main gate at the center of the west wall, and a smaller gate on the east side. The commandant's house was in the center, a chapel along the east wall, and the interior walls were lined with stables, warehouses, and eventually, homes for some of the soldiers.

Tucson artist Cal Peter's conceptual drawing of the Royal Spanish Presidio in Tucson, circa 1795. View looking southeast. (Courtesy of Arizona Historical Society, 597 15)

The practical mission of the Tucson presidio was to counter the threat of Apache raiders. Captain Pedro Allande became commandant of the fort in 1777, and through 1784, defended the presidio against four direct

Apache attacks and conducted relentless campaigns against the Apache in their own territory.

In the mid-1780s, Spain adopted a new Apache policy by encouraging the natives to settle near presidios and trading posts, where they would be "rewarded" with food rations, spirits, and (inferior) weapons. The plan worked - for the first time there was peace on the frontier. Tucson acquired its first Apache residents in 1787, when about 100 men, women, and children built their wickiups beside the Santa Cruz River at the northern end of the presidio.

Spanish settlers, attracted by the relative safety of the Tucson presidio, soon arrived to farm the banks of the Santa Cruz River, to mine in the surrounding hills, and to graze cattle. Spanish and Native American farmers grew corn, wheat, vegetables, and cultivated fruit orchards in irrigated fields. Foreshadowing future problems, there was competition for water, leading to agreements that increasingly favored the presidio residents over the Native Americans.

For the last 30 years of the Spanish empire in Mexico (1790-1821), the Santa Cruz Valley and Tucson flourished. Awe-inspiring churches were built at the missions of San Jose de Tumacácori and San Xavier del Bac. A massive two-story *convento* (general purpose building) was built near the Mission San Agustin del Tucson along with a four-acre walled garden to supply fruits and vegetables to the presidio and adjoining natives.

Tucson's population grew slowly, reaching about 1,000 in 1819, including a full complement of about 100 soldiers, plus Native Americans, settlers, and priests.

But big changes were brewing. Spain, the world's richest and most powerful nation, was in decline and its empire was breaking up; European wars had taken their toll. In 1810 Mexicans started a revolution to achieve their freedom. Finally in 1821 the Mexican War of Independence ended with Mexico free after 300 years of Spanish colonialism.

Mexican Period

After achieving independence, Mexico suffered a financial depression. Frontier colonization efforts suffered greatly, including those in the Santa Cruz Valley and the Tucson presidio. There was a shortage of men and resources. The presidio fell into disrepair. Church buildings were neglected, including Mission San Agustin del Tucson, abandoned in 1831, and the majestic *convento*, finally abandoned in 1843.

Mission San Agustin's convento (shown around 1900) gradually melted away after Spanish rule ended. (Tom Marshall photo courtesy of Patricia Stephenson)

Old alliances between Spain and the natives ended. There were no rations for the peaceable Apaches, so they left the proximity of the Tucson presidio and resumed raiding. Meanwhile the population of the peaceful O'odham natives in the Santa Cruz Valley was declining drastically due to diseases brought by the Europeans and Apache depredations.

The Mexican economy slowly improved. Mexico continued Spain's policy of providing land grants in southern Arizona, drawing new farmers and ranchers. Mexicans also claimed abandoned O'odham lands adjoining the missions along the Santa Cruz River - a veritable "land grab," according to anthropologist Thomas E. Sheridan.

Mexico encouraged trade with the "western" United States; soon trade routes were established between Missouri settlements and New Mexico, and eventually southern Arizona. Fur trappers started operating along Arizona rivers in the 1820s; some visited Tucson. Tucson was beginning to be noticed by the United States.

By the mid-1840s, the Mexican depression was over and Mexican Army forces occupied the Tucson presidio.

Farming continued as the main Tucson industry. Additional Mexican settlers began arriving from the south. Winter crops of wheat, barley, chickpeas, lentils, and garlic followed the summer crops of corn, beans, squash, pumpkins, chili peppers, tobacco and cotton. Irrigation schedules were set by an elected overseer. Mexican ranchers irrigated cattle pastures in the valley south of Tucson.

In 1846 Mexico went to war with the land-hungry United States over disagreements about the ownership of Texas and California. American forces quickly occupied New Mexico and California and then mounted a resupply mission to California from New Mexico. That expedition - the first to use wagons on a transcontinental journey - was accomplished by the famous Mormon Battalion under Lieutenant Colonel Philip St. George Cooke. They passed through Tucson and then westward along the Gila River on the trail traveled 70 years earlier by Juan Batista de Anza.

The Mexican-American War ended in 1848 with Mexico ceding lands to the U.S. for $15 million that included Texas and the future states of California, Utah, Colorado, Wyoming, New Mexico, and the part of Arizona north of the Gila River.

Contacts between Mexican Tucson and Americans increased dramatically when gold was discovered in California in 1848. Tens of thousands of American gold seekers traveled west through Tucson in 1849 and 1850 to reach the California gold fields.

Soon a growing colony of Americans had settled in Tucson - attracted by local mining and ranching possibilities. Tucson was transforming to a small town. Development - including homes, businesses and stores - had expanded outside the walls of the presidio. Apaches were still a menace but stayed away because of the troops. According to Tucson historian C. L. Sonnichsen, Tucson was "Not a bustling town yet, but it was beginning to stir."

In 1854, completing a deal to secure lands for a southern transcontinental railroad, the United States Congress approved the Gadsden Purchase; the U.S. paid Mexico $10 million for southern Arizona.

Tucson now belonged to America!

Tucson in U.S. Territory
1854 to 1912

On June 29, 1854 the U.S. Congress approved the Gadsden Purchase in which the U.S. acquired southern Arizona, including Tucson, from Mexico. The new lands were added to the New Mexico Territory, created in 1850 following the Mexican-American War. Mexican troops remained in Tucson to keep peace until United States troops took charge in 1856.

New Mexico Territory

According to Tucson historian C. L. Sonnichsen, "Tucson was still a Mexican village in the late 1850s." But, the Americanization of Tucson was about to pick up the pace. Starting before the Gadsden Purchase, in 1853, and continuing through 1855, American surveyors crisscrossed southern Arizona through Tucson looking for suitable paths for a transcontinental railroad. By 1857 Texas-California stagecoaches started traveling through Tucson, truly putting the village on the American map.

American prospectors rediscovered old Spanish and Mexican mines along the new border with Mexico. Big ranches operated successfully in the Santa Cruz Valley.

The "great transition" of Tucson was beginning. Business was good and the village was growing with an 1859 inventory that included three stores, two butcher shops, two blacksmith shops, and at least two drinking establishments. The 1860 census counted 623 people including newcomers from all sections of the U.S. and 12 foreign countries. The walls of the old presidio were rapidly being dismantled, although the final standing portion lasted until 1918.

But the 1860s brought violence to southern Arizona and Tucson. Apache raids against ranches suddenly increased. American reprisals made things worse as 25 years of "Apache wars" began. The U.S. Civil War also started in 1861; the U.S. was forced to withdraw soldiers from Arizona to fight in New Mexico and back East. This left Arizona defenseless against the fierce Apache.

Turbulence increased when the Confederate States of America claimed that southern Arizona was part of Confederate territory in mid-1861. Confederate troops actually "captured" Tucson in early 1862 and later that year skirmished with Union troops at Picacho Peak, before withdrawing from Arizona in mid-1862, leaving Tucson in federal jurisdiction.

Tucson, with all of Arizona, remained part of the New Mexico Territory until February 23, 1863 when President Abraham Lincoln signed legislation creating a separate Arizona Territory by splitting the New Mexico Territory along a north-south line (instead of an east-west line). Southern Arizona and southern New Mexico were thought to favor the Confederacy so this action would break up a potentially hostile bloc.

Prescott, not Tucson, was the first capital of the new Arizona Territory. Tucson was regarded as too supportive of the Southern Cause.

Arizona Territory

After the Civil War ended in 1865, Tucson resumed a major role in campaigns to fight the Apache. A military supply depot formed in 1862 near the center of town, was expanded and reestablished as Camp Lowell in 1866, and then in 1873 moved to a new location a few miles east of town at the confluence of Pantano and Tanque Verde Creeks, and commissioned as Fort Lowell. The installation provided supplies and manpower to outlying military installations.

Journalist J. Ross Browne's sketch of Tucson in 1864. (Courtesy of Arizona Historical Society, 91791-B882t)

Hundreds of Tucson militia served in expeditions against the Apaches. In 1871, a group of Tucson citizens became so upset with the deaths from Apache raids, that they took matters into their own hands in what became known as the Camp Grant Massacre to attack a peaceful group of Apaches about 50 miles northeast of Tucson, killing 130 people, mostly women and children. The debilitating wars with the Apache continued until 1886, when Apache leader Geronimo finally surrendered.

In a political war, in 1867 Tucson successfully lobbied the governor of the Arizona Territory to move the Arizona capital from Prescott to Tucson. This was in exchange for Tucson supporting the governor's ambition to be a delegate to Washington. The territorial capital remained in Tucson a decade until 1877, when unhappy Prescottonians succeeded in recovering "the coveted prize."

By 1870, transcontinental stagecoach service through Tucson, which had been discontinued during the Civil War, was resumed between the East and California. Tucson also became the hub for local stagecoaches and freight wagons trading with Mexico and serving mining communities within a hundred miles of town.

Tucson was incorporated in 1871, becoming a municipality with a mayor and four councilmen. For the first time land titles were issued; property ownership became certain.

The 1870s saw Tucson's first public schools, the first public library, the debut of the *Tucson Citizen* and *Daily Bulletin* (forerunner of the *Arizona Daily Star*) newspapers, and the development of several mercantile stores.

Sonnichsen wrote, "by 1877 [Tucson] had two hotels, a county courthouse, a United States depository [document library], two breweries, two flour mills, four feed and livery stables, and ten saloons. ... Tucson had become the largest and most important community in Arizona Territory." Census records record the growth of Tucson from 3,224 in 1870 to 7,007 in 1880.

Much of Tucson's business growth in this period was due to Mexican immigrants who became some of Tucson's leading citizens and whose entrepreneurial efforts resulted in prosperous freighting, stagecoach transportation, and merchandizing businesses.

As anthropologist Thomas E. Sheridan wrote, "Underlying everything ... was the pervasiveness of Mexican culture. ... The strongest representatives of Mexican culture in this fragile bicultural society were the Mexican woman who married Anglo men."

Meanwhile the population of relatively peaceful Native Americans in and around Tucson was dwindling due to disease and mistreatment by the increasing numbers of Anglos and Mexicans. U.S. policy was to concentrate the natives on a few reservations. In 1859 a reservation for the Akimel O'odham (Pima) was established to the north of Tucson, along the Gila River. In 1872 a reservation was finalized for the Apache in the White Mountains. And in 1874 a Tohono O'odham (Papago) reservation was established south of Tucson, west of the Santa Cruz River, encompassing Mission San Xavier del Bac.

The southern route of the transcontinental railroad reached Tucson in 1880. Tucson was on the "main line" and was in good position to support expanded mining and ranching efforts in southern Arizona. Settlers were now able to reach Tucson in large numbers – effectively ending the southern Arizona frontier.

As anthropologist Sheridan put it, "Prior to the railroads, Arizona looked south [to Mexico] for much of its business and many of its goods. ... People could almost hear the axis of money and power shifting from north-south to east-west."

Tucsonans experienced more "firsts" in the 1880s, including Saint Mary's Hospital, gas lighting, electricity, the telephone, the Tucson Fire Department, the University of Arizona, the Tucson Water Department, and the Arizona Historical Society.

Water was about to become a big problem for Tucson. For centuries the Santa Cruz River had flowed almost year round. Reservoirs were built to impound River waters for farming, gardening, and to power flour mills. New, deep ditches for irrigation and four years of natural flooding in the late 1880s and early 1890s effectively ruined the old irrigation system. Soon, wells to tap ground water were being dug all over metropolitan Tucson; this would have far reaching consequences.

St. Mary's Hospital was one of many "firsts" for Tucson in the 1880s. (Postcard image courtesy of Al Ring, circa 1908)

An economic depression began in Arizona in the late 1880s and lasted for ten years. All major industries were affected, including mining and cattle ranching. Sonnichsen described the difficult times, "Business was so bad in Arizona that the population of Tucson, its largest city, declined in 1890 to a little over 5,000 ... Tucson was actually for the moment, shrinking."

The difficult time was made worse by a sustained period of lawlessness in the form of stagecoach and train robberies, gunfights on the streets of Tucson, murder, rape, robbery, and out of control gambling.

A slow economic recovery and reform efforts improved the situation in Tucson. In the late 1890s, the first locally owned automobile appeared on Tucson's (still) dirt roadways, and streetcars pulled by mules were in service. New residences and businesses were built along an ever-widening perimeter around Tucson. By 1900 the population of Tucson had recovered to over 7,500.

Tucson's growth continued in the early 1900s. A new industry - the health industry - was blossoming. There was a rush of health-seekers to Tucson, looking to the warm, dry climate to heal tuberculosis and other respiratory ailments. And tourists were discovering Tucson and it fabulous weather! Guest ranches and resorts were born. By 1910 Tucson's population reached just under 14,000.

In 1910 Congress Street (looking west) was still not paved but was the principal roadway in downtown Tucson. (Courtesy of the Arizona Historical Society, B32948)

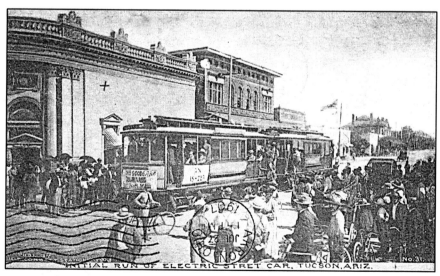

Tucson's first electric streetcar run occurred in 1906. (Postcard image courtesy of Al Ring)

On February 14, 1912, President William Howard Taft signed the documents that admitted Arizona as the 48th U.S. state. Even though Tucson had more people, Phoenix was designated as the state capital, because of its central location.

In 58 years, Tucson had transitioned from a Mexican village of a few hundred people to a sizeable American town. The population mix in 1912 was about 55% Anglos (proportion growing rapidly) and 40% Mexicans.

But, Tucson's most significant growth was yet to come.

Tucson in the State of Arizona
1912 to the Early 21st Century

When Arizona became a state on Valentine's Day, February 14, 1912, five different flags had flown over Tucson: Spanish, Mexican, United States, Confederate, and now the State of Arizona.

1912 to 1940

Tucson continued its steady, if not spectacular, growth from a town of about 14,000 (1910 census). Municipal services such as water, electricity, and gas; paved streets; and public transportation transformed the community's quality of life. The automobile and electric streetcar expanded residential neighborhoods outside the business district. The "look" of the town changed as brick and substantial, multistory stone buildings replaced low, flat-roofed adobe buildings.

The look of Sentinel Peak changed also as students from the University of Arizona in 1916 painted a 70 x 160 foot letter "A" on the hillside, thereby christening "A-Mountain."

During World War I in 1917 and 1918, Tucsonans weathered vigorous efforts to increase production of vital war materials like copper and supported conservation activities like food-savings programs. Adding to the stress, there was concern about the possibility of Germany invading

Arizona through Mexico, severe labor-relations confrontations with the pacifist union, Industrial Workers of the World (affecting mining of copper), and the onset towards the end of the war of the great influenza epidemic.

Foreshadowing Tucson's long aviation history, in 1919 the first municipally owned airport in the United States opened on land that is now the site of the Tucson Rodeo Grounds. Later, in 1927 the airport was moved to the current site of Davis-Monthan Air Force Base and dedicated by famed aviator Charles Lindbergh.

Famed pilot Charles Lindbergh came to Tucson to dedicate the new municipal airport on September 23, 1927. (Courtesy of the Arizona Historical Society, B94401)

Tucson was the largest city in Arizona until the 1920 Census where the population of Phoenix at 29,050 exceeded Tucson's at 20,300.

The 1920s were mostly prosperous for Tucson. Civic leaders continued to improve the city's social, educational, cultural, and economic institutions. The Tucson Museum of Art and the Tucson Symphony were founded.

The Tucson Sunshine Climate Club promoted tourism, selling Tucson's spectacular climate, weather, and Old West attributes. In doing so, the club coined the "Old Pueblo" moniker for Tucson and repeated it so often in advertising that the name "stuck."

Dude ranches, fine hotels, and medical clinics proliferated. Tucson's first two skyscrapers, the Pioneer Hotel and the Consolidated Bank Building, were completed in 1929.

The Pioneer Hotel on the northeast corner of Stone Avenue and Pennington Street around 1950. (Postcard image courtesy of Al Ring)

But then the stock market crashed; the Great Depression of the 1930s affected Tucson dramatically. Construction, farming, and mining jobs disappeared. Businesses and banks failed. Generally, it was hard for Tucsonans to support their families. The Federal government provided much-needed jobs building a dam in Sabino Canyon and the Mount Lemmon Highway.

The 1930s also saw the end of irrigation farming along the Santa Cruz and Rillito Rivers. After centuries of perennial flow, increased water usage and pumping ground water since the 1890s had dried up both the above ground and underground river flows.

Tucson received national notoriety in 1934 when the famous outlaw John Dillinger and his gang were captured after gang members fled from a fire in the downtown Hotel Congress and police found Dillinger in a nearby rental home.

Towards the end of the 1930s business began to recover and new jobs were created. Tucsonans experienced gasoline powered buses, air conditioning, and the first shopping center at Broadway Village.

Tucson's Congress Street looking west in 1931. *(Postcard image courtesy of Al Ring)*

By 1940 the population of Tucson had grown to over 35,000 - about two-thirds Anglo and one-third Hispanic, mostly of Mexican heritage.

1940 to the Early 21st Century

In 1940 Tucson began to increase pumping of groundwater, the growing city's only water source for decades to come. The amount of water taken out of the ground aquifer exceeded what nature could replace (recharge from rain and snow melt). By the 1980s, the water table had dropped more than 200 feet in some places and some land areas had sunk, drawing water away from riparian areas.

Tucson had a major role in military training during World War II (1941-1945). Davis-Monthan field became a U.S. Army Air Base. Thousands of pilots were trained there; at Ryan Field, west of town; and at Marana Air Base, to the north. Marana Air Base, activated in 1942, trained 10,000 pilots by the end of the war, becoming the largest pilot-training center in the world. Besides pilots, infantry and cavalry detachments were stationed in or near Tucson for training for desert warfare in Africa and testing military equipment.

In 1943 Consolidated Vultee Aircraft (later Convair division of General Dynamics) built three huge wooden hangars for B-24 Liberator modifications on the future site of Tucson International Airport.

In the late 1940s, Tucson's municipal airport was moved from Davis-Monthan field to its current location, eventually becoming Tucson International Airport. The initial airline terminal was at one end of the old Consolidated Vultee hangars. (These gigantic hangars are still present today and can be leased for storage space.)

The Army Air Base became Davis-Monthan Air Force Base, and as its military role expanded, emerged as one of Tucson's largest employers. One of the AFB's missions - extended storage of military aircraft - is unique to Tucson, because of our dry climate and alkali soil. Starting in 1945, out-of-service aircraft have been lined up in the desert "boneyard," awaiting possible return to operational status or providing spare parts - until disposal of spent airframes. Approximately 4,200 aircraft are stored there today.

Tucson experienced tremendous growth in the 1950s. The population increased fourfold, from 55,000 in 1950 to almost 213,000 in 1960. Reasons for the huge growth rate included increased manufacturing with new industries relocating to Tucson, a huge increase in tourism leading to a construction boom, the permanent return of servicemen who were trained in Tucson during World War II, and even the wide use of air conditioning that made desert life so much more pleasant year round.

One of the keystone industry startups during this period was Hughes Aircraft Company which in 1951 built a new manufacturing plant aside the Tucson International Airport. Initially manufacturing radar units, the company gradually transitioned to producing military missiles, becoming the premier missile builder in the U.S., and today as Raytheon Missile Systems, is Tucson's second largest employer.

The 1960s in Tucson started with a business slow-down but the population still expanded rapidly because of a "tidal wave" of immigration. The percentage of Anglos in Tucson, which had been increasing for years, peaked near 80% and began to decline as the percentage of Hispanics increased - a trend continuing to this day.

Business began to pick up by the mid-1960s. The big copper mines that ringed the town expanded and stepped up production. Nearby enterprises like Titan missile sites and the astronomical observatory at Kitt Peak added to Tucson's economy. Construction of the I-10 and I-19 freeways started in the 1960s and completed in the 1970s. New industries came to town, including International Business Machines in 1978.

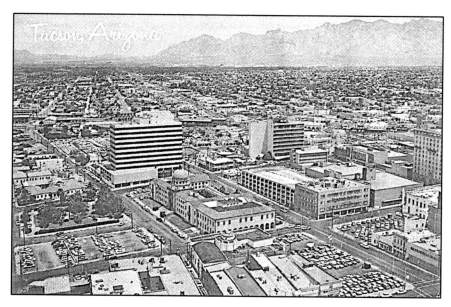

Tucson in 1966. (Postcard image courtesy of Al Ring)

Meanwhile another critical Tucson problem - the supply of water - was being addressed. Over a period of 20 years, starting in 1973, the Central Arizona Project built a 336-mile diversion canal from the Colorado River to Tucson and in 1992 started providing water to Tucsonans to supplement the limited ground water. After resolving some CAP water-quality problems, in 2001 Tucson began blending CAP water and underground water. In an effort to conserve water, today Tucson is recharging groundwater with some of the CAP water.

Tucsonans also began historic preservation efforts. Designation of historic neighborhoods began in 1976 and continues today. In 1999 voters approved the Tucson Origins Heritage Park project to begin partial restoration and interpretation the Tucson Presidio and San Agustin de Tucson Mission Gardens. In the 2000s a 2 ½ mile historical walking tour of downtown Tucson – The Presidio Trail – was completed.

As Tucson entered the 21st century, the University of Arizona led an advanced technology business revolution in Tucson with numerous lunar and planetary spacecraft and astronomy programs that make the UA Tucson's largest employer today. Roughly 150 Tucson companies are involved in the design and manufacture of optics and optoelectronics systems. Another emerging high-tech industry in Tucson is biosciences – including hospitals, medical device firms, and drug research companies. Tucson has become well known for its care of heart and cancer patients and its responsive trauma centers.

Recreation was not neglected in Tucson. Rillito River Park, 500 miles of metro bicycle paths, 300 miles of mountain biking trails, more than 120 parks (including Saguaro National Park), and innumerable golf courses and mountain hiking trails attract both residents and visitors. Tourism is now a $2 billion a year business with 3.5 million visitors annually. Four casinos in the Tucson area - owned and operated by Native

A rendering of the Phoenix Mars Lander. The program was headed by the UA Lunar and Planetary Lab. (Courtesy of Wikimedia Commons)

Americans - provide gaming opportunities. Annual events like bicycling's Tour de Tucson, the Gem and Mineral Show, and the Tucson Rodeo are nationally known and widely attended.

The city of Tucson's metropolitan population was just over 520,000 at the 2010 census, with the growth rate slowing. The proportion of Hispanics (41.6%), compared to Anglos (47.2%) continues to grow. More people are settling outside the city as the 2010 population of metropolitan Tucson approached a million people.

Facing the Future

Tucson faces serious problems for the future. From the 1970s, there has been steady growth in smuggling of illegal drugs from Mexico. Illegal immigration across the Mexican border started to increase dramatically in the 1990s. For years, Tucson's downtown has been in urgent need of urban renewal and planning for business development. These issues still persist.

Other issues confronting Tucson today include public transportation and deteriorating Tucson roadways. The tragic shooting death of U.S. Congresswoman Gabriele Giffords in a Tucson shopping center in early 2011 sparked increased concern over gun control and psychiatric screening. Environmentalists are upset about proposed new mining near Tucson.

Water conservation - saving what Tucson has and providing for the future - remains as perhaps Tucson's greatest challenge. Will Tucson's allocation of CAP water from the Colorado River support continued Tucson growth? More basic perhaps, will the Colorado River continue to provide enough water to satisfy all its many customers in the southwestern United States?

Tucsonans have always faced severe challenges - from 11,000 years ago as wandering hunter-gatherers, through the last 4,000 years or so in permanent settlements along the Santa Cruz River, perhaps the longest continuous human presence anywhere in the U.S. That impressive history offers hope for a bright, if uncertain, future.

Chapter 2

Influential Tucson Pioneers

For Tucson's early history, through Arizona's Territorial Period, here are my selections of Tucson's most influential Mexican, Anglo American, and Jewish pioneers.

Mexican Pioneers

Tucson's first non-native permanent residents were Spanish soldiers and Franciscan missionaries who moved into the new Tucson presidio in the fall of 1776. After a decade of almost continuous fighting against fierce nomadic Apaches, peace was established under a new Spanish policy that encouraged the Apache to settle near presidios in return for food rations. Spanish settlers, attracted by the relative safety of the Tucson presidio, soon arrived to farm the banks of the Santa Cruz River, to mine in the surrounding hills, and to graze cattle.

The Spanish were able to essentially "partner" with resident Pimas and Tohono O'odham along the Santa Cruz River, initially working out farmland and irrigation agreements, and using these more sedentary Native Americans as an early warning system against hostile Apaches. For decades Tucson prospered with the population slowly growing.

After Mexico achieved its independence from Spain in 1821, an economic depression curtailed the support to Apaches settled around the Tucson presidio; Apaches resumed raiding ranches in southern Arizona. As difficult economic times eased, Tucson saw the beginning of Anglo American immigration - mostly people passing through - like trappers, California gold seekers, military men, and transcontinental route explorers.

When the U.S. took over Tucson in 1854 with the Gadsden Purchase, Tucson was still a Mexican village of perhaps 500 people. As anthropologist Thomas E. Sheridan wrote in his book *Los Tucsonenses*, "[Mexicans] and their descendants continued to raise families and run businesses in southern Arizona. They became cattlemen, freighters, Indian fighters, and merchants. They built schools, erected churches, established newspapers, and enforced the law. Without them, territorial Tucson could never have been created. They helped transform a little finger of Sonora into a commercial center of the southwestern United States."

Anglos who prospered did so in partnership with Mexicans and catered to the larger Mexican population. The two groups treated each other with respect in mutually interdependent relationships. Anglos and Mexicans joined Pima and Tohono O'odham Indians in expeditions against their common enemy - the Apache. During the period before the arrival of the Southern Pacific Railroad, Tucson was according to Sheridan, "a unique bi-cultural and bi-ethnic" town.

Historian Manuel G. Gonzales, in his book *Mexicanos*, notes that "The most lucrative economic endeavor in the 1860s and 1870s was long-distance freighting. ... Tucson was ideally suited to service both the pueblos of Sonora ... and the New Mexican settlements along the Rio Grande."

Tucson blossomed in the 1870s. By 1880 Tucson's population exceeded seven thousand, with 70% Mexican.

The coming of the railroad in 1880 reoriented most of the major commercial routes through Tucson from north and south to east and west. This effectively ended the lucrative wagon freighting connection with Mexico and stimulated a mining boom in southern Arizona that required enormous amounts of capital from East and West Coast business interests. Historian Gonzales wrote that, "The advent of corporate capitalism spelled disaster for the Mexican entrepreneurs of Tucson." Tucson was changing from an agricultural economy to an urban center.

The Mexican population of the Arizona Territory was overwhelmed by the huge influx of newcomers from the East. These Anglos were less tolerant of cultural diversity than their predecessors and realized that there was less to gain by cultivating good relations with Mexicans.

After a decade of economic depression in the 1880s - with a significant decline in population - and a decade of recovery in the 1890s, the population of Tucson had increased to just over 7,500, but the percentage of Mexicans had dropped to 45%.

Anthropologist Sheridan summed up the situation as Tucson approached the end of the nineteenth century, "[Mexican business people] found themselves serving one segment - the Mexican one - of a society growing more and more dualized, and more and more segregated, with each passing year."

Jesús Maria Eliás (1829-1896) was born in Tubac to a family long prominent in Sonora. He was a rancher and farmer and was also active as a tracker and Indian fighter, having lost six members of his family to Apache raiders. He served as an army guide in 1863 in a successful attack on Apaches in Aravaipa Canyon, and was the leader of the 1871 Camp Grant Massacre where a group of vigilantes from Tucson annihilated a group of peaceful Apaches, mostly woman, children, and elders. Eliás served in three Territorial Legislatures as a representative from Tucson and Pima County.

Pedro Aguirre (1835-1907) was born in Chihuahua, Mexico, one of three brothers whose father in 1852 set them up in Las Cruces, New Mexico in a freighting business along the Santa Fe Trail between Missouri and New

Mexico. The brothers moved to Arizona in the late 1850s to start a freighting business from Tucson to Yuma and Sonora. While American mining was developing along the border with Mexico, in 1870 Pedro Aguirre started the Arizona & Sonora Stage Line in Tucson to carry mail and passengers between Tucson and Altar, Sonora Mexico, with connections southward to the Sonoran capital, Hermosillo, and the important Gulf of California port at Guaymas. The Aguirre brothers also entered the livestock business, running thousands of head of cattle from Casa Grande to Sasabe. Pedro Aguirre established a ranch west of Arivaca that now is the headquarters of the Buenos Aires National Wildlife Refuge. He also helped establish the Arivaca Land and Cattle Company.

Estévan Ochoa (1831-1888) was "The most respected of the Arizona traders," according to historian Gonzales. Ochoa was born in Chihuahua,

like the Aguirre brothers, and for a while partnered with them in trading along the Santa Fe Trail. Ochoa came to Tucson in 1860 and partnered with Anglo Pinckney Randolf Tully in a freighting business that became the most successful and one of the largest freighting firms in Arizona. Company operations extended to Kansas and included retail stores in Tucson and surrounding towns. Mining, sheep raising, and stagecoach lines also contributed to Ochoa's fortune. During the Civil War and the occupation of Tucson by Confederate forces, Ochoa left Tucson rather than

Estévan Ochoa was the most respected of Arizona traders. (Courtesy of findagrave.com)

swear allegiance to the Confederacy, expressing instead his steadfast loyalty to the country to which he had immigrated. After the war, Ochoa returned to Tucson to resume his businesses. Estévan Ocha was a generous philanthropist and an influential community leader, encouraging public education and other civic improvements. Ochoa represented Pima County in three Arizona Territorial Legislatures, and was elected as Tucson's mayor in 1875, the only Mexican to hold the position in Arizona's territorial period. Historian Gonzales wrote about the effect of the railroad on Ochoa's operations, "The arrival of the locomotive brought the collapse of his freighting empire and cost him his fortune, but it did not diminish Don Estévan's immense popularity with his fellow citizens, Anglo as well as Mexicans." As difficulties began to arise for Tucson's Mexican population, Ocha helped form the town's first Mexican mutual-aid society.

Tucson's first public school was built on the corner of Congress Street and Sixth Avenue in 1875. The land and $5,000 needed for construction were donated by businessman Estévan Ochoa. (Courtesy of UA Special Collections, 655)

Mariano Samaniego (1844-1907) was born in Bavispe, Sonora into a multi-generation well-to-do family. Before the Gadsden Purchase, Samaniego worked in his widowed mother's mercantile establishment in Mesilla, New Mexico. Then he attended college, graduating from Saint Louis University. Like Pedro Aguirre and Estévan Ochoa before him, Samaniego started a freight line - Samaniego's operating from New Mexico as far east as the Mississippi River. Just before he moved to Tucson in 1869, Samaniego married a daughter of the Aguirre family – thus joining the two influential families. In Tucson Samaniego continued freighting, ran a harness shop, became a cattle rancher, and developed a modern irrigation system. Foreseeing implications of the transcontinental railroad, in 1881 Samaniego sold out his freighting business and concentrated on his other businesses. Records show that in 1887 Samaniego was a member of the Tucson Volunteer Fire Department. From the early 1890s to the early 1900s Samaniego ran his own stagecoach service to Arivaca and Oro Blanco, mining towns south of Tucson. He is acknowledged as the most influential Tucson citizen in the 1890s. He served four terms in the Territorial Assembly, terms on the County Board of Supervisors, Tucson City Council, and as Pima County Assessor. Samaniego was one of the founders of the Hispanic American Alliance, a major Mexican mutual aid society, served on the first Board of Regents for the University of Arizona, and was President of the Arizona Pioneers' Historical Society.

Leopoldo Carrillo (1836-1890) was born in Moctezuma, Sonora and moved to Tucson in 1859. Like Ochoa and Samaniego, he was a long-distance freighter for a time. Within ten years Carrillo was one of the most prominent businessmen in Tucson and its most successful urban entrepreneur. He built the first ice cream parlor, bowling alley, two-story building, and fired-brick building. He was a member of the first School Board and established the Republican Party in Tucson. Carrillo owned several homes, nearly 100 houses that he rented as landlord, a ranch west of the Santa Cruz River and another at Sabino Canyon. The Federal census in 1870 identified Carrillo as the wealthiest person in Tucson. In 1885 Carrillo opened a fabulous public park in Tucson, Carrillo Gardens, with eight acres, featuring three spring-fed ponds with two boats. The Gardens, about a quarter-mile southwest of downtown (at today's South Main and West Simpson Streets), had 500 peach trees, 2000 grape vines, 200 quince trees, 60 pomegranate trees, and nine apricot trees. The rose garden was one of the finest in Tucson. The Gardens also had 12 bath houses, a saloon, shooting gallery, restaurant, dancehall, zoo, and circus.

Carlos Velasco (1837-1914) was born in Hermosillo, Sonora. He was educated as a lawyer, became a judge in 1857 at the age of 20, and won a seat in the Sonoran legislature two years later. His meteoric political career in Sonora was interrupted by a series of destructive government conflicts and Velasco became a political refuge, forced to flee to the United States in the mid-1860s. He came to Tucson, worked in his brother's general store for a few years, returned to Mexico in the early 1870s, again became disenchanted with the government, and returned to Tucson to stay in 1877. Velasco was an intellectual who soon became a crusader for the rights of Mexicans living in the United States. In 1878 he started a Spanish-language newspaper, *El Fronterizo*, that championed Mexican causes, and lasted for 36 years. In 1894 Velasco was the major founder (supported by Mariano Samaniego and at least 40 other prominent Hispanics) of the Hispanic American Alliance that supported Mexican economic and political objectives.

Anglo American Pioneers

Before the Gadsden Purchase, approved by the U.S Congress in 1854, that brought Tucson into American territory, the only Anglo Americans in Tucson were transients: beaver trappers (beginning in the 1820s), military personnel from the Mormon Battalion (1846), Argonauts on their way to the California Gold Rush (1849, 1850), and government surveyors exploring future transcontinental wagon and railroad routes (1840s/1850s).

In the mid-1850s Americans from the East and the West Coast came to Arizona to mine silver in the mountains just north of the new border with Mexico. These miners and people traveling on transcontinental stagecoaches through Tucson (starting in 1857) began to put Tucson on the American map. Soon a growing colony of Anglos had settled in Tucson – attracted by mining prospects, ranching possibilities, and business opportunities.

Business was good – especially the freighting business and the mercantile stores that sold what the freighters brought to Tucson. Tucson's business inventory included butcher shops, blacksmith shops, and saloons. Anglos worked with Mexicans in harmony and often in partnership.

The 1860 Tucson census counted 623 people (5% Anglo) including newcomers from all sections of the U.S. and 12 foreign countries. Tucson was just beginning the decades-long transition from a Mexican village to an American town.

Census records show the growth of Tucson (and the proportion of Anglos) from 3,224 (15% Anglo) in 1870 to 7,007 (25% Anglo) in 1880.

The southern route of the transcontinental railroad reached Tucson from the west in 1880 and was completed to the east during 1881. The large number of Anglo settlers now reaching Tucson helped change Tucson from a Mexican agricultural economy to an Anglo urban center.

An economic depression began in Arizona in the late 1880s and lasted for ten years. The population of Tucson actually declined in 1890 to a little over 5,000.

Tucson's slow population growth resumed in the 1890s, but the mix of Mexicans and Anglos was changing rapidly. By 1900 Tucson's population had recovered to just over 7,500; the Anglo population had grown to equal the Mexican population (about 45% each) and continued to increase proportionally.

The transcontinental railroad came to Tucson in 1880 (depot shown in 1890s), accelerating the transformation of Tucson from a Mexican agricultural town to an Anglo urban center. (Courtesy of UA Special Collections, N11,058)

Tucson's political situation had also been evolving. The Arizona Territory was separated from New Mexico in 1863. The capital of Arizona was moved to Tucson for a decade in 1867. Beginning in the Arizona Territorial Assembly in 1891, continuing through Constitutional Conventions, and introduction of numerous bills in the U.S. Congress, officials pushed long term efforts that eventually succeeded with Arizona statehood in 1912.

President William Howard Taft signs the bill that made Arizona the 48th state in 1912. (Courtesy of Library of Congress)

Solomon Warner (1811-1899) was born in Warnerville, New York. He worked on a Mississippi river boat, joined the California Gold Rush in 1849, worked in Nicaragua, and then San Francisco in 1853, before his work as a mason took him to Fort Yuma in 1855. He changed careers again to become a merchant, leading a 13-mule train loaded with merchandise to Tucson, arriving in 1856 just about the time Mexican troops permanently withdrew from the area. Warner partnered with Mark Aldrich from Illinois, later to become Tucson's first American mayor, to open a store, becoming the first merchants to sell goods made in the United States. Warner prospered as a shopkeeper until the Civil War, when he refused to take a loyalty oath to the Confederacy during the southern troops' brief occupation of Tucson, and fled to Santa Cruz, Sonora, where he met and married a wealthy widow. After the War Solomon returned to Tucson and using his wife's money, expanded his business ventures to include farming and cattle ranching. During a journey from Santa Cruz to Tucson in 1870, he was wounded by Apache and permanently crippled. In 1874/1875 Warner built a flour mill, and a small dam to power it, along the Santa Cruz River. The mill proved to be unprofitable and he shut it down in 1881. Oddly, Warner spent his final years attempting to build a perpetual motion machine.

William Oury (1817-1887) was born in Virginia, moved with his father to Texas, at the age of 19 escaped the Alamo (under siege by Mexicans) as a courier, fought with Sam Houston against General Santa Anna, became a Texas Ranger, and fought in the Mexican War with the Texas Volunteers. After the War, Oury married a Mexican woman, moved to San Francisco, then headed south and east to arrive in Tucson in 1856. Oury acquired a small cattle ranch on the Santa Cruz River, worked as the agent for the Butterfield Overland Mail Company until operations stopped at the start of the Civil War, and was a respected citizen and community leader. Oury was an ardent secessionist but did not take up arms during the War. However, he did take up arms in two duels, killing his opponent in both instances. With Sylvester Mowry - soldier, miner, and tireless worker for an independent Arizona - he bought Arizona's first newspaper, the *Tubac Arizonan*, and moved it to Tucson. Oury participated in several expeditions against the Apache and in 1871, along with Jesús Maria Eliás, led the force from Tucson in the Camp Grant Massacre. Oury's political career included being appointed as the first mayor of the village of Tucson in 1864, member of the School Board in 1867, appointment as Alderman when Tucson was incorporated in 1871, member of the Tucson City Council in 1872/1873, and Pima County Sheriff from 1873-1876. He was also the first president of the Arizona Pioneers' Historical Society in 1887.

Hiram Stevens (1832-1893) was born in Vermont, where he worked briefly as a farmer, then in 1851 enlisted in the army, fought against the Apache in the New Mexico Territory, and after his discharge, settled in Tucson in 1856. Stevens operated a ranch near Sentinel Peak and in 1858 began a series of business partnerships with Samuel Hughes. Stevens married Petra Santa Cruz, whose father and grandfather had been born inside the old presidio. From 1866-1872 Stevens supplied Fort Buchanan and later Fort Crittenden (near Sierra Vista) with trading goods. In 1876 Stevens and Hughes formed the Hughes, Stevens & Company that was active in cattle, mercantile, and mining interests. Stevens became one of the richest men in the Arizona Territory. Stevens also excelled in politics, serving as Tucson city treasurer, Pima County tax assessor, and was a member of

Hiram Stevens was a respected Tucson politician and businessman, becoming one of the richest men in Arizona Territory. (Courtesy of Wikimedia Commons)

the Pima County Board of Supervisors on numerous occasions. He was also the second president of the Arizona Pioneers' Historical Society. The respected politician served two terms in the Territorial Legislature and twice as Territorial Arizona's Delegate to the U.S. Congress. Stevens and his wife frequently entertained Washington officials and other prominent guests in their beautifully furnished Tucson home. Suffering a downturn in his business interests, and under "severe mental distress," Stevens died of a self-inflicted gunshot wound.

Samuel Hughes (1829-1917) was born in Wales, immigrated to Pennsylvania with his parents in 1837, and from there went to California during the Gold Rush and became a merchant. Hughes contracted tuberculosis and while traveling east seeking a drier climate, made an unscheduled stop in Tucson in 1858, where he recovered his health and began a retail butchering business. When Confederate Forces occupied Tucson during the Civil War, he moved back to California, leaving his business interests in the hands of his partner Hiram Stevens; he later returned to Tucson with Union troops. Hughes and Hiram Stevens became brothers-in-law when Hughes married Atanacia Santa Cruz, Petra Santa Cruz's younger sister. This self-educated man became one of Tucson's leading and most influential citizens. In the early 1870s, Hughes helped to incorporate Tucson and became an Alderman on the first Tucson City Council. In 1871 he helped early territorial governor A.P.K. Safford establish public education in the Arizona Territory. Also in 1871 he helped plan (but did not participate in) what was later called the Camp Grant Massacre. Hughes served several terms on the Tucson School District No. 1 Board during the 1880s and at other times was Pima County Treasurer and held important positions in the territorial government. He was an organizer of the Arizona Pioneers' Historical Society in 1884, serving as president and director. In his later years, Hughes was active in mining, real estate, and civic works.

Pinckney Randolph Tully (1824-1903) was born in Mississippi, moved with his family - first to Arkansas, then to Missouri, drove a herd of sheep to California in 1849, before returning to the Santa Fe Trail and partnering with Estévan Ochoa in a wagon freighting business with headquarters in Las Cruces, New Mexico. He brought a wagon train to Tucson in 1858 and sold everything to Solomon Warner within a few hours. In 1866 Tully opened a store in Tucson and by 1868 had joined Ochoa and settled permanently in the old pueblo, helping Ochoa run their increasingly profitable Tully & Ochoa freighting business. Tully also served his community, twice as Mayor of Tucson, four years as Territorial Treasurer, Tucson City Treasurer, Tucson City Councilman, and a member of the Tucson Board of Health. He supported many public causes, particularly education and activities of the Catholic Church. In 1877 Tully founded two newspapers in Tucson - the *Daily Bulletin*, partnering with Louis C. Hughes, and the Spanish-language *Las Dos Repúbicas*. In 1879 Tully sold his interest in the *Bulletin* to Hughes. The *Repúblicas* only lasted two years, but confirmed that there was a market for a Spanish-language newspaper in Tucson. (Mexican immigrant Carlos Valasco started his long-lasting Spanish-language newspaper the next year in 1878.) In 1881 Tully helped propose a streetcar line for Tucson, but the project died and Tucson had to wait until 1898 for mule-drawn streetcars. In his later years Tully concentrated on support to education, aiding in the establishment of a parochial school.

Robert Leatherwood (1844-1920) was born in North Carolina, fought in the Confederate army, and came to Tucson in 1869, where he opened a stable in the downtown area that became known throughout the southwest. His impressive public service record included City Councilman, several-time member of the state legislature, 12 years as Pima County Sheriff, County Treasurer, and captain of the Arizona Rangers who went out after Geronimo in 1876. Leatherwood was mayor of Tucson in 1880 when the transcontinental railroad reached Tucson. He worked hard to prepare Tucson for the railroad, including helping to sell $10,000 of bonds to pay for the depot and yards demanded by Southern Pacific. From 1886-1892 Leatherwood was a member of the Tucson Volunteer Fire Department. He was later in charge of building a gravity water system for the city of Tucson. Leatherwood was short and thin, but "the little giant" was a feisty resident of Tucson and in his later years, a colorful pioneer representative of the town - both at home and in travels around the U.S. At his request, he was buried in his Confederate uniform.

Louis C. Hughes (1842-1915), younger brother of Samuel Hughes, was born in Philadelphia, orphaned in 1845, indentured to a "Calvinist farmer" at age 10, gained his release at age 16, briefly served in the Union army toward the end of the Civil War, then worked as a machinist, and studied

law. Hughes married Josephine Brawley in 1868, and because of health concerns, moved to Tucson in 1871 where he opened a law practice. In 1872 he was selected as a member of the Tucson City Council, then appointed a probate judge, and elected Pima County Attorney. In 1873 Hughes was appointed by Territorial Governor Safford as Attorney General for the Arizona Territory. In 1877 he stopped practicing law full time, and began publishing a newspaper, the *Daily Bulletin*, with partner Pickney Randolf Tully. In 1879 Hughes took over full ownership of the paper and renamed it the *Arizona Daily Star*. As a liberal

Louis Hughes founded the Arizona Daily Star and served as Governor of Arizona. (Courtesy of Wikimedia Commons)

Democrat, Hughes and his influential wife pushed for the deportation of indigenous Apaches to Florida, and opposed liquor and gambling, while championing higher education and the women's suffrage movement. Hughes was Governor of the Arizona Territory from 1893-1896, while his wife ran the newspaper in his absence. In 1897 Hughes returned to Tucson from Phoenix (where the capital had been since 1889) and resumed publishing the *Star.* He favored joint statehood with New Mexico, but lived to see New Mexico and Arizona become independent states in 1912.

Jewish Pioneers

At the same time Christopher Columbus was "discovering America" in 1492, Spain expelled all Jews who wouldn't convert to Catholicism. During the 16th century some of these Jews fled to Mexico, but when the "Inquisition" crossed the Atlantic to Spanish Mexico, outlawing the Jewish faith there, Jews who wanted to continue their religious practices had to do so in secret as so-called "crypto-Jews." Over generations, some Jews fled north to frontier Spanish settlements in south Texas and New Mexico. According to Jewish historian Harriet Rochlin, even after Spanish rule ended in 1821, Jews (along with other non-Catholics) in the Mexican West "were denied landownership, citizenship and public worship" and "treated with suspicion."

With American rule after the Mexican War in 1848 and the Gadsden Purchase in 1854, came religious freedom and legal equality for Jews. As historian Rochlin wrote, "Finding possibilities and access unlimited, they [Jews] summoned relatives and friends to join them, first in gold-rush California, then elsewhere on the erupting frontier."

With the end of the Civil War in 1865 and the transfer of the Arizona territorial capital from Prescott to Tucson in 1867, business opportunities in Tucson abounded.

The Jewish Virtual Library summarizes the beginning of Jewish heritage in Tucson:

> "At first there were relatively few people, Jews and gentiles, in the community, but some Jews came because of merchandising opportunities. Some opened general stores, others acquired Indian trading licenses, and some also served as contractors for the U.S. Army. The settlement in the 19th century consisted mostly of young men out to seek their fortunes. ... The total Jewish population of Arizona in the 1880s was estimated at about 50 people, so the numbers in Tucson must have

been fewer. [The population of Tucson in 1880 was about 7,000.] A number of men from the city's pioneer Jewish families ... could be found in elected political positions: on the school board, on the county Board of Supervisors, and even as mayor."

Jews in territorial Tucson were also miners, bankers, and prominent in the entertainment business.

Jewish family businesses were common in Tucson. In 1878 for example, as Tucson merchandising historian Bettina Lyons observed, of the ten general stores operating in downtown Tucson, "six were owned by first generation German Jews, all related to one another by either blood or marriage."

There were virtually no single Jewish women in early territorial Arizona, so Tucson's pioneering Jewish men often had to travel "back" East or to the West Coast to meet and marry Jewish women.

There were no rabbi's in Arizona until the 1900s, so lay leaders took on the responsibility of presiding at Jewish religious ceremonies.

With the coming of the railroad in 1880 and the amassing of financial resources in fewer hands, opportunities for individual entrepreneurs declined. The Jewish Virtual Library says of Tucson, "Many of the original Jewish settlers fled to other parts of the West or the nation in the late 1880s and 1890s when an economic depression hit the Arizona territory."

Brothers **Philip Drachman** (1833-1889) and **Samuel Drachman** (1837-1911) were among the earliest Jews to settle in Tucson, became successful businessmen, and helped keep Judaism alive in the desert southwest. The brothers were born in Russian-occupied Poland and immigrated to New York City in 1852. Philip immediately headed west where he lived first in California and then the Yuma area, exploring farming, stock raising, and merchandising. By the mid-1860s Philip had established general stores in Yuma and Prescott with his partner Isaac Goldberg, and by 1866 had settled in Tucson and entered the retail business. Meanwhile, Samuel had gone from New York City to Charleston, South Carolina and later fought for the Confederate army during the Civil War. At the invitation of Philip, Samuel came to Tucson in 1867, where he worked for his brother at the Drachman-Goldberg general store until 1873, when he established his own business as a government contractor carrying supplies and mail. Both Drachman brothers successfully sought out Jewish wives, Philip traveling to New York and Samuel to California.

Philip Drachman, one of the first Jews to settle in Tucson, became a successful business and helped keep Judaism alive in the desert southwest. (Courtesy of Southwest Jewish Archives)

Besides merchandising, Philip Drachman bought and sold real estate, operated an extensive freighting business between Tucson and Yuma, opened a saloon, and purchased a cigar store - often operating more than one business at a time. Philip also represented Pima County in the 4th Territorial Legislature before his death in Tucson from pneumonia. One of Philip's sons, Mose Drachman, became a prominent Tucson businessman in the early 1900s. Another of Philip's sons, Emanuel, was the father of Roy Drachman, one of Tucson's key developers and civic leaders in the mid and late 1900s.

Like his brother, Samuel Drachman also engaged in multiple businesses, including a cigar store, agent for principal lottery companies, insurance agent, and railroad ticket broker. Samuel also served in the Arizona's 8th Territorial Legislature and was heavily involved in the development of Tucson's school system. During his entire life in Tucson, Samuel Drachman served as lay leader to Tucson's Jews, often presiding at local religious ceremonies, especially weddings.

Brothers **Louis Zeckendorf** (1838-1937) and **William Zeckendorf** (1842-1906), together with their nephew Albert Steinfeld, established one the most successful and longest lasting merchandising businesses in Tucson. Louis and William were born in Germany, along with their older brother, Aaron. By 1856 the three brothers were merchants and army provisioners in New Mexico. In 1866, Aaron and Louis decided to open a new store in Tucson with younger brother William in charge, older brother Aaron to manage their New Mexico business, and Louis to move to New York City to purchase goods for the Zeckendorf enterprises. The Tucson store opened with Philip Drachman as temporary manager. When William arrived in 1867, he struggled in managing the store, preferring to gamble and participate in self-serving promotions and spectacles. In 1870 Aaron Zeckendorf closed the New Mexico business to concentrate Zeckendorf efforts in Tucson. When Aaron died unexpectedly in 1872, Louis Zeckendorf took over as head of the family business and although visiting Tucson frequently, brought in his 17-year-old nephew Albert Steinfeld to help him make a better go of the sole remaining Zeckendorf brothers operation.

L. Zeckendorf & Co. at Tucson's Main and Pennington Street, ca. 1880. Albert Steinfeld, with hand on hip, is standing in front row (center) below wall lantern. (Courtesy of Bettina Lyons)

Meanwhile, William pursued other interests; on his second try in 1875 he was elected as a member of the 8th Arizona Territorial Legislature. Also in

1875 William married the daughter of a successful New York City clothing merchant. As Zeckendorf biographer Lyons says, by this time "William Zeckendorf was considered one of Tucson's 'upstanding citizens.'" He and his wife were popular and entertained often in Tucson.

In 1878 William resigned from the family enterprise and opened a store of his own that thrived for a while but suffered due to overextended credit and competition from inexpensive goods arriving by rail after 1880. While his business struggled, William invested heavily in mining in Pima and Santa Cruz Counties, and devoted much of his time to managing Arizona's Democratic Party. William's business finally failed in 1883, later reopened on a less grand scale, but closed for good in 1891 when, with his mine speculations failing, William sold off his entire stock and joined his family in New York City, where he lived for the rest of his life.

Albert Steinfeld took over as managing general partner of L. Zeckendorf & Co. in 1878 when William resigned. Except for occasional visits, Louis Zeckendorf was able to remain in New York City. Steinfeld survived the coming of the railroad, actually grew the business (with the help of financial advisor Charles M. Strauss, another German Jew), and in 1904 bought out Louis Zeckendorf to become sole owner. Steinfeld turned Albert Steinfeld & Company into the largest, most elegant, and most successful department store in the territory - and which thrived in Tucson until the 1980s.

Jacob S. Mansfeld (1832-1894) founded Tucson's first bookstore and the first public library, and was instrumental in getting the University of Arizona started. Mansfeld was born in Pasewalk, Germany, came to America in 1856, and worked in bookstores in San Francisco, California; Virginia City, Nevada; and White Pine, Nevada before arriving in Tucson in 1869. Mansfeld opened the Pioneer News Depot and Bookstore, selling newspapers from New York City, magazines, and books. The shop also sold stationery and other writing materials. In 1871 Mansfeld established the first public library in town, loaning books from his store.

In 1878 Mansfeld found and married a Jewish woman in New York City. One of their four children, Monte (changed name to Mansfield), became a prominent Tucson auto dealer and civic leader in the 20th century.

Mansfeld helped draft the first charter for the City of Tucson as a member of the county Board of Supervisors from 1885-1886. In 1886, as one of four original regents for a proposed territorial university, he successfully raised money, found a site, and secured land to build the University of Arizona. Mansfeld was also a School Board member from 1888-1891.

Brothers **Lionel Jacobs** (1840-1922) and **Barron Jacobs** (1846-1936) were successful Tucson merchants and started the first bank in town. The brothers were sons of a Polish Jew who migrated with his family to San Francisco, California in 1851. The brothers clerked there in the family clothing and dry goods store until 1867, when their father sent them to Tucson to open a new store. The brothers rented an empty building from established merchant and Mexican immigrant Leopoldo Carrillo and launched a small mercantile firm. The business was supplied from San Francisco by the brothers' father via a challenging logistics path over water and land - the final leg on freight wagons from Yuma. The Jacobs' merchandising business grew and prospered through the 1870s.

Lionel and Baron were active in Tucson social life and civic affairs. They helped form the Tucson Literary Society in 1873. Lionel found a Jewish wife in San Francisco and Baron in New York City. Lionel was appointed to the Pima County Board of Supervisors in 1871, was elected to the 7th Territorial Legislature, was Treasurer of the Territorial Legislature in 1873, and also served on the Tucson City Council. Baron also served as Treasurer of the Territorial Legislature.

Starting in the 1870s, more and more of the Jacobs brothers business involved handling money. In 1871 they established a loan business in the store. The next move was to start a money exchange operation, where gold coin from San Francisco was exchanged for paper money in Tucson. By 1879 the exchange enterprise was so profitable that the brothers organized the Pima County Bank, the first banking institution in Tucson.

Over the years, through a series of mergers and consolidations, the Pima County Bank eventually became Valley National Bank, controlled and directed by the Jacobs' family until 1935.

Alex Levin (1834-1891) was Tucson's first pioneer in the entertainment business. Levin was born a Jew in Germany and made his way to Tucson in 1869 where he started the Pioneer Brewery. He soon purchased Wheat's Saloon, arranging for music and dancing, and in 1870 took over the Hodges Hotel. Over the next decade Levin turned his brewery grounds into a three-acre park (at the corner of today's Granada and Congress Streets), adding a dance hall, restaurant, an opera house that seated 2,000 people, a shooting gallery, archery range, an icehouse, a bath house, riding stables, and a bowling alley. Levin's Park was very popular and in its heyday, into the 1880s, it was the location of every important and communal event in Tucson - until the much larger Carrillo Gardens opened in 1885 and Levin's Park declined.

In 1884 Alex Levin was a Tucson City Councilman.

Unlike many Jewish men, Levin married a Mexican from a prominent family in Sonora, and adopted his wife's Catholic faith. Levin family descendants include internationally known singers Luisa Espinel and Linda Ronstadt.

Charles M. Strauss (1840-1892) was Tucson's first Jewish mayor and an early proponent of the University of Arizona. Strauss was born into a Jewish family in New York City, studied finance, and worked in Boston, Tennessee, and Ohio, finding a Jewish wife in Memphis, Tennessee in 1868. The Strauss family came to Tucson in 1880, seeking a beneficial climate. Strauss worked for Albert Steinfeld as business manager of the Zeckendorf general store, improving the store's accounting and stocking procedures. Almost immediately, Strauss found himself on Tucson's School Board, joined Tucson's new Volunteer Fire Department in 1882, and was elected Tucson's Mayor in 1883, but resigned in 1884 when a political dispute arose. During his abbreviated term, he did much to transform the appearance of Tucson, shepherding the construction of a city hall, a firehouse, an infirmary, a stand-alone library, a building and loan association, and graded roads. Strauss and his wife became extremely active in Tucson's social activities; their home became a center for culture including literary and music programs. In 1886 Strauss was elected Territorial Superintendent of Public Instruction. Perhaps his greatest achievement to Tucson's legacy was his work in 1886 with fellow Jew Jacob Mansfeld to sell bonds to buy land and start construction of the University of Arizona.

Jacob S. Mansfeld and Charles M. Strauss were instrumental in securing land and raising money to start construction of the University of Arizona. The first building was Old Main shown here in 1889. (Courtesy of History of Arizona)

Chapter 3

Tucson's Movers and Shakers

For the period of Arizona's transition to statehood and the years afterward, here are my choices for Tucson's movers and shakers in business, politics, arts and entertainment, science and medicine, and sports.

Business

Movers and shakers in business enabled the growth and development of Tucson. Beginning in the late 19th century, **Fred Ronstadt**, helped Tucson through its transition from a territorial agricultural village to an awakening Arizona industrial town by evolving his business from carriage making to hardware and farm equipment to providing automobiles. Son of Jewish territorial pioneer, Jacob A. Mansfeld, **Monte Mansfield**, a Ford dealer for 44 years, was pivotal in bringing Davis-Monthan Air Force Base to Tucson, establishing our civilian municipal airport, and in convincing Howard Hughes to establish Hughes Aircraft in the our city – these events building the backbone of Tucson's aerospace industry. Great nephew of territorial pioneer Philip Drachman, corporate real estate developer **Roy Drachman**, regarded by many as "the most influential person who ever lived here," was key in building Tucson's first shopping centers, arranged the land deals that brought Hughes to Tucson, and was instrumental in bringing major league baseball to Tucson. Finally, "Renaissance man" **John P. Schaefer** - academic, astronomer, photographer, and conservationist - led the University of Arizona as president for a dozen years, accelerating the development of Lunar & Planetary Sciences and Astronomy - technology efforts that enabled the UA to grow into today's largest Tucson employer.

Fred Ronstadt (1868-1954), son of a German immigrant to Mexico, was born in Sonora Mexico and came to Tucson in 1882 to learn the blacksmithing and wheelwright trades. He formed the F. Ronstadt Wagon and Carriage Company to manufacture wagons, buggies, harnesses and saddles - for just about everybody in town. When the automobile came to Tucson in the early 1900s, Ronstadt added an Oldsmobile dealership to his operation. Following World War I Ronstadt dropped the automobile business, and under the F. Ronstadt Hardware and Machinery Company, concentrated on farm tools, tractors, leather goods and water pumps, and added general hardware, becoming the largest business of its kind in southern Arizona - lasting into the 1980s.

Fred Ronstadt was also an active community leader. He served a two-year term on the Pima County Board of Supervisors, was active in Chamber of Commerce work for almost 50 years, and supported numerous political campaigns and causes.

Ronstadt's cultural legacy is music. A guitarist and vocalist, he taught many Tucsonans to play instruments, founded Tucson's first professional orchestra, the Club Filarmonico Tucsonense in 1896, and helped organize the Tucson Symphony Orchestra in the 1920s. Ronstadt's granddaughter is the internationally acclaimed singer, Linda Ronstadt.

Monte Mansfield (1884-1959) was the son of Jewish German immigrant Jacob Mansfeld, who opened Tucson's first bookstore and library and was instrumental in getting the UA started. Monte Mansfield was born in Tucson, attended the UA (without graduating), started a Ford dealership in 1917, and added the "i" to his last name in 1923.

The first of Mansfield's contributions to his generally acknowledged reputation as "the man who played the greatest role in Tucson's growth" occurred in 1935, after more than 10 years of strenuous effort, with the opening of the Stone Avenue underpass. As Chairman of the State Highway Commission, Mansfield was able to replace many of Tucson's rutted dirt roads with paved roads. Just before the start of World War II, acting for the Chamber of Commerce, Mansfield convinced officials in Washington DC to locate Davis-Monthan field in Tucson. In 1948, when it became apparent that the City didn't have the resources to operate the new civilian airport, Monte Mansfield led 15 municipal leaders to form the Tucson Airport Authority,

As president of the Tucson Airport Authority, Monte Mansfield helped establish Davis-Monthan AFB and bring Hughes to Tucson. (Courtesy of Tucson Rodeo Parade)

raising money and paving the way for aviation in Tucson. In 1951 as president of the Tucson Airport Authority, Mansfield worked with four other local businessmen to bring Hughes Aircraft Company to Tucson. Finally, in 1958, after 44 years of operations, Mansfield sold his Ford dealership to Holmes Tuttle.

Over the years Mansfield also served a term on the Tucson City Council, was president of the Tucson Chamber of Commerce, the Arizona Pioneers Historical Society, and the Arizona Automobile Dealers' Association.

Roy Drachman (1907-2002) was born, raised and educated in Tucson. His grandfather Philip Drachman was among the earliest Jews to settle in

Tucson and became a successful businessman. When his father Emanuel Drachman became seriously ill, Roy Drachman left the University of Arizona to manage his father's theater business. In 1939 Drachman became manager of the Tucson Sunshine Club to promote tourism and Tucson's healthy climate. Thereafter, he raised the funds that established Tucson Medical Center. Before being drafted into World War II, Drachman helped sell six million dollars in war bonds.

Roy Drachman developed Arizona's first shopping centers and helped put together land deals to attract Hughes Aircraft Company to Tucson. (Courtesy of findagrave.com)

After World War II, in 1946 Drachman established his own real estate brokerage business. He partnered with developer Del Webb and sold houses for Webb in Tucson's first large housing development. Also with Webb, he co-developed the first shopping centers in Arizona. He put together the land deals that attracted Hughes Aircraft to Tucson. Drachman also helped found the Ramada Inn hotel chain.

Drachman, who played semi-pro baseball, was key in bringing major league baseball spring training to Tucson. He also helped launch the Conquistadors, hosts of the Tucson Open Golf Tournament.

Roy Drachman's devotion to civic duty included being a staunch supporter of the UA, helping raise funds for the Medical School, and over his lifetime donating three million dollars to the university.

Drachman wrote two books, *This is Not A Book: Just Memories* and *From Cowtown to Desert Metropolis: Ninety Years of Arizona Memories*, chronicling nearly 100 years of growth in Tucson.

John P. Schaefer (1934-) was born in New York City to German immigrants. He earned a PhD in chemistry at the University of Illinois, did post-doctoral work at the prestigious University of California at Berkeley, began teaching there in 1959, and came to the lesser-known UA in 1960, attracted by the challenge of making the university a regional and national presence.

Schaefer had a meteoric career at the UA – first research and teaching, later leading the Chemistry Department and College of Liberal Arts, and finally serving as University President from 1971-1982. While Schaefer was president, he started the Department of Lunar and Planetary Sciences and supported the development of the Mirror Lab. These efforts helped spawn numerous U.S. space probes, and mirrors and associated telescope programs that enabled the UA to grow dramatically. Schaefer also guided UA and Arizona State into the PAC-10 Conference.

Following his 21 years at the UA, Schaefer continued his passion for astronomy by joining the Research Corporation for Science Advancement as president and was a key player in developing one of the world's most advanced optical telescopes, the Large Binocular Telescope, now operational atop of Mount Graham, near Safford. Next, Schaefer became the chairman of the nonprofit corporation overseeing the development of the "most significant" Large Synoptic Survey Telescope, scheduled to be mapping the universe twice a week in 2022 from a mountaintop in Chile.

John Schaefer has also published six books on photography and was the founder, with friend Ansel Adams, of UA's renowned Center for Creative Photography. As a conservationist he helped organize the Tucson Audubon Society and The Nature Conservancy in Arizona. His tireless community support includes the Arizona-Sonora Desert Museum, the Tucson Museum of Art, and many other arts and social service groups.

Politics

Tucson's movers and shakers in politics include two former mayors and two members of the U.S. House of Representatives. Norwegian immigrant **Henry Jaastad** was a seven-term mayor who led Tucson through difficult times in the 1930s and 1940s. As Tucson's longest term mayor, in the 1970s and 1980s **Lewis C. Murphy** oversaw a time of economic and population growth. Rancher and social activist **Isabella Greenway** was the first U.S. Congresswoman in Arizona history and in 1930 founded the Arizona Inn. Respected trial lawyer **Morris Udall** served 30 years in the U.S. Congress, earning a reputation as the "most creative and productive legislator of the 20th century."

Henry Jaastad (1872-1965) was born in Norway, immigrated to the United States in 1886, and arrived in Tucson in 1902 as a journeyman carpenter. He formed his own contractor business, became a naturalized citizen in 1904, completed correspondence courses in architecture and studied electrical engineering at UA, and in 1922 earned his architecture license. Starting as a designer of small residential buildings for private individuals, Jaastad branched out into commercial ventures including stores and office buildings in downtown Tucson, plus schools, churches, and hospitals, earning him accolades as the designer of "some of Tucson's most significant public architecture," until his retirement in 1957, having been responsible over his 50-year career for over 500 projects. Jaastad buildings still existing include Tucson High School and several buildings at Tucson Medical Center.

Jaastad was also actively involved in local politics, serving two terms as a City Councilman in 1925/26 and 1931/32, then seven terms as democratic Mayor of Tucson from 1933 to 1947. His political service spanned Tucson's recovery from the Great Depression through the end of World War II, maintaining the financial integrity of the city with a "pay as you go" approach. Jaastad helped to secure natural gas from New Mexico, the Stone Avenue underpass, 90 miles of paved streets, public pools at city parks, and expansion of military airfields at Davis-Monthan and Marana.

As writer Mona L. McCroskey put it, "Henry Jaastad's work as an architect and his tenure as mayor have left an indelible imprint upon the City of Tucson."

Lewis C. Murphy (1933-2005) was born in New York City, grew up in Iowa and Minnesota, moved to Tucson in 1950, earned a business degree from UA in 1955, served as a U.S. Air Force pilot in Japan from 1955 to 1958, and then returned to Tucson to earn a law degree in 1961. He spent the 1960s in private practice and banking and was appointed Tucson's City Attorney in 1970.

"Lew" Murphy, a Republican, was elected Tucson's mayor in 1971 and served 16 years through four terms until 1987, assisted during most of that time by City Manager Joel D. Valdez, and guided Tucson through many changes. The City's population nearly doubled and high-tech companies such as IBM and Learjet (now a subsidiary of Bombardier) opened plants in Tucson. Murphy brought CAP water to Tucson, started the Community Food Bank, built a route to the airport, and annexed 63 square miles of additional land for the city.

Murphy "truly loved the community" and regarded the best part of being mayor as getting to meet people.

Isabella Greenway (1886-1953) was born Isabella Selmes on a farm in Kentucky, attended schools in New York City where she met and became lifelong friends with Theodore Roosevelt's niece, Eleanor, and was one of Eleanor's bridesmaids when she married Franklin Roosevelt.

In 1923 Isabella married Col. John Campbell Greenway, who brought Isabella to Arizona, to a ranch near Bisbee, where he was manager of the Calumet and Arizona Mining Company. In 1927, a year after her husband died suddenly, Isabella moved her family to Tucson. That same year, using money from selling her copper stock, Isabella bought a ranch in Williams, Arizona and a year or so later, became owner and operator of Los Angeles-based Gilpin Airlines.

Isabella Greenway was elected as Arizona's representative to the 73rd U.S. Congress, blazing a trail for remarkable woman in Arizona politics. (Courtesy of Wikimedia Commons)

Isabella's political activities intermixed with her successful entrepreneurial operations, blazing a trail for remarkable women in Arizona politics today. During the late 1920s, in Tucson, she opened a furniture factory employing disabled veterans and their immediate families. In 1928 she became Arizona's Democratic National Committeewoman, and in 1932 she campaigned heavily for Franklin Roosevelt. Greenway was elected as Arizona's sole Representative to the 73rd Congress in 1932 and won reelection in 1934, working to improve Arizona's economy, provide employment, expand irrigation and flood control, improve roads, and protect veterans' benefits.

Meanwhile, in 1929/1930, Greenway built Tucson's Arizona Inn - greatly enhancing Tucson's reputation as a tourism destination. The Arizona Inn is considered among the top hotels in the world - still active today and in the National Register of Historic Places.

Morris Udall (1922-1998) was born in St. Johns, Arizona, lost his right eye in a childhood accident, served in the Army during World War II, graduated from UA where he was a star basketball player, played basketball professionally for the Denver Nuggets for a year, and then returned to UA to earn a law degree in 1949, after which he quickly established a record as a great trial lawyer, particularly in personal injury law.

In 1961 "Mo" won a special election for his brother's vacant seat in the U.S. Congress, when Stuart Udall was appointed Secretary of the Interior in the Kennedy administration. Mo Udall was reelected 13 more times as a democrat, championing environmental causes, campaign finance reform, and the welfare of Native Americans, until he resigned in 1991 due to the effects of Parkinson's disease. In 1976 he ran unsuccessfully for the Democratic nomination for President as a liberal alternative to Jimmy Carter.

Morris (Mo) Udall championed environmental causes, campaign finance reform, and the welfare of Native Americans. (Courtesy of Wikimedia Commons)

As a Congressman, Morris Udall authored the Alaska Lands Act of 1980, which doubled the size of the National Park System, as well as legislation to protect archaeological finds, enact civil service reform, legalize Indian casinos, and provide for the safe disposal of radioactive waste. He was respected for his vision and integrity - even by Republicans.

Arts and Entertainment

Movers and shakers in arts and entertainment include an architect, an artist, an author-historian, and a musician. **Josias Joesler** is Tucson's "most recognized architect," who in the 1930s and 1940s designed 400 buildings. **Ted DeGrazia**, the "world's most reproduced artist," is renowned for his western paintings and sculpture, especially colorful images of Native American children. Among more than 30 books, mostly on southwestern history and folklore, **C. L. Sonnichsen** wrote the acclaimed definitive history of the old pueblo, *Tucson: The Life and Times of an American City*. Granddaughter of Tucson business mover and shaker, Fred Ronstadt, immensely successful popular-music singer **Linda Ronstadt**, "blessed with arguably the most sterling set of pipes of her generation," has been an "inspiration for every aspiring young singer" in our town.

Josias Joesler (1895-1956) was born in Zurich, Switzerland, educated in history and architecture in Germany and France, lived in Spain a while, and then worked as an architect in Havana, Mexico City, and Los Angeles, before coming to Tucson in 1927.

Joesler initially worked with builder John W. Murphey and his decorator wife Helen who were trying to build residential communities that would attract wealthy clients from the East "to the resort desert city of Tucson." Innovations included non-gridiron street patterns, southwestern architecture, and landscaped lots.

Many of Joesler's residential buildings are in the Catalina Foothills Estates and the Blenman-Elm neighborhood (just east of UA Medical Center) listed in the National Register of Historic Places.

Most of Joesler's work reflects a Spanish Colonial Revival style. His buildings utilized traditional southwestern hand applied plaster, hand hewn beams, colored concrete floors, and decorative iron/tin work. Besides residences, memorable Joesler extant buildings include Broadway Village (Tucson's first shopping center), Saint Philips-in-the-Hills Episcopal Church, St. Michael and All Angels Episcopal Church, the Arizona History Museum, Fourth Avenue Shops, Ghost Ranch Lodge, and the Hacienda Del Sol reconstruction – a true architectural legacy for Tucson.

Ted DeGrazia (1909-1982) was born Ettore DeGrazia to Italian immigrants in Morenci, Arizona, graduated from Morenci High School, eschewed a life as a copper miner, moved to Tucson in 1932, worked his way through the UA to earn Bachelor's degrees in Art Education and Fine Arts, and later went back to UA to earn a Master's degree in Art Education in 1945.

In the late 1930s DeGrazia began creating his early paintings. In 1942 *Arizona Highways* magazine started to publish his images, many based on his impressions from extensive travel throughout southern Arizona and northern Mexico. In 1942 DeGrazia went to Mexico City to work for both Diego Rivera and Jose Clemente Orozco, two of Mexico's most famous artists.

Ted DeGrazia is renowned for his western paintings and sculpture. (Courtesy of Wikimedia Commons)

Back in Tucson in the mid-1940s, and finding that no galleries were interested in displaying his work, DeGrazia built his own small gallery in Tucson, and then in 1951 bought 10 acres of land in the foothills east of Tucson and built his *Gallery in the Sun* [6300 North Swan], "still standing today as a testament to the man and his work."

Other galleries finally began showing DeGrazia's work. In the early 1950s he seriously started working on ceramics. In 1960 UNICEF chose his image of Los Ninos (the children) for their Christmas card and DeGrazia's popularity and success exploded.

C. L. Sonnichsen (1901-1991) was born Charles Leland Sonnichsen in Fonda, Iowa, graduated from high school in Minnesota, earned a BA in English at the University of Minnesota and a Masters and Ph.D. in English at Harvard. Sonnichsen spent 41 years at the Texas College of Mines and Metallurgy as a researcher, teacher, Chairman of the English Department, and Dean of the Graduate School, before arriving in our town in 1972, at age 70, becoming "a Tucsonan by adoption."

Sonnichsen was Director of Publications and Editor of the *Journal of Arizona History* from 1972-1977, then Senior Editor until his death in

1991. "Dean of southwestern historians," he combined self-taught research with an admired light-hearted writing touch in 34 books. His comprehensive history of Tucson, published in 1982, "chronicles with humor and affection the growth over two centuries of one of the region's most colorful communities."

Linda Ronstadt (1946-) was born in Tucson, grew up in a musical family, learned to play the guitar, and attended Catalina High School, before leaving to go to Los Angeles where she became part of the Stone Poneys folk trio that released its first album in 1967. By the end of the 1960s, Ronstadt was a solo act, releasing several albums before 1974's "Heart Like a Wheel" achieved platinum status, i.e., sold more than a million copies.

Linda Ronstadt has earned numerous awards, including 11 Grammy's, over her career. (Courtesy of Wikimedia Commons)

Ronstadt quickly became a musical superstar. She had success with many different styles, including rock, rock and roll, folk, country rock, jazz, Latin American, Cajun, big band, pop rock, art rock, and operetta. Her diversity led to collaborations with other musical greats including Billy Eckstine, Rosemary Clooney, Emmylou Harris, Dolly Parton, Neil Young, Johnny Cash, and Nelson Riddle. In total Ronstadt has released over 30 studio albums and 15 compilations of greatest hits, earning 11 Grammy Awards, two Academy of Country Music Awards, an Emmy Award, an American Latino Media Arts Award and numerous gold, platinum, and multiplatinum album certifications.

Ronstadt's ties to Tucson continued over her career. She often brought recording business back to Tucson and still owns a home here, keeping in touch with childhood friends.

In 2013 Linda Ronstadt was diagnosed with Parkinson's disease, which left her unable to sing. In April 2014 Ronstadt was inducted into the Rock and Roll Hall of Fame.

Science and Medicine

Tucson's movers and shakers in science and medicine include an archeologist, a planetary scientist, a heart transplant surgeon, and a pioneer in integrative medicine. **Emil Haury** was a preeminent archaeologist and anthropologist who accumulated the evidence that provides much of our understanding of southwestern prehistory. **Michael J. Drake**, a "world-class scientist" in extraterrestrial geology, was director of UA's lunar and planetary projects, and was instrumental in several successful NASA space missions. While at UA, **Jack Copeland** performed Arizona's first heart transplant and later pioneered the use of artificial hearts to temporarily "bridge a patient to heart transplant." **Andrew Weil** is a medical pioneer in treating both the mind and body for a healthy life.

Emil Haury (1904-1992) was born in Newton, Kansas, educated in Kansas through two years of college, then transferred to UA where he earned a Bachelor's degree in archaeology in 1927 and a Masters in 1928, and later a PhD from Harvard University in 1934.

Haury began his archaeological field work in the late 1920s, exploring prehistoric ruins in northern Arizona and Mexico, and in 1930 became the Assistant Director of the Gila Pueblo Archaeological Foundation in Globe, working for Harold Gladwin. With Gladwin's support, Haury was instrumental in identifying and defining the Hohokam culture in Arizona and the Mogollon culture in New Mexico, which flourished around AD 1000 and earlier. Haury also became a key figure in developing tree-ring

Emil W. Haury was instrumental in defining the Hohokam and Mogollon cultures. (Courtesy of Wikimedia Commons)

dating that enabled construction of event timelines for prehistoric sites. In the 1940s and 1950s Haury excavated numerous ancient (circa 9,000 B.C.) Paleoindian Mammoth Kill Sites in Arizona and New Mexico.

In 1937 Haury returned to UA to head the Department of Anthropology and a year later became the Director of the Arizona State Museum, holding both posts until 1964.

The National Academy of Sciences summarized Emil Haury's contributions, "… a perceptive researcher and a master teacher, a skilled administrator … He surveyed more [greater Southwest landscapes], excavated more sites in it, observed more details of its prehistory, and gained a more sensitive perspective of its problems than any of his contemporaries."

Michael Drake (1946-2011) was born in Bristol, England, graduated with a degree in geology from Victoria University in Manchester, and received a PhD in 1972 from the University of Oregon. After postdoctoral studies at the Smithsonian Astrophysical Observatory in Cambridge, Massachusetts, he joined the faculty of UA's Planetary Sciences Department in 1973 as an assistant professor.

In 1994 he became the Head of the Department of Planetary Sciences and the Director of the Lunar and Planetary Laboratory (LPL), serving until his death in 2011. Under Drake's leadership, LPL grew from a small group of geologists and astronomers into a "powerhouse of research into the solar system."

Drake played a key role in a number of high-profile space projects that garnered international attention for LPL and UA. Those include the Cassini mission to explore Saturn, the Gamma-Ray Spectrometer onboard NASA's Mars Odyssey Orbiter, the HiRISE camera onboard NASA's Mars Reconnaissance Orbiter, and the Phoenix Mars Lander. He had over 100 peer-reviewed scientific papers published in his career.

Drake was principal investigator of the most ambitious UA planetary science project to date - the NASA mission to retrieve a sample of an asteroid and return it to earth to study the origins of life – to be launched in 2016.

Jack Copeland (1942-) was born in Roanoke, Virginia, earned a medical degree from Stanford in 1969, did his internship and residency at the University Hospital in San Diego, served with the National Heart and Lung Association at Bethesda, Maryland, and then returned to Stanford where he became Chief Resident of General Surgery.

Dr. Jack Copeland performed Arizona's first heart transplant at Arizona Medical Center. (Courtesy of American Heart Association)

UA hired Copeland from Stanford in 1977 to head UA's Cardiovascular and Thoracic Surgery Program. "Pushing the frontiers of research and new techniques," Copeland and his team performed Arizona's first heart transplant in 1979 and produced the first successful bridge to heart transplant with a total

73

artificial heart in 1985. Copeland also became a leader in heart valve surgery and coronary bypass surgery. In 33 years at UA, he performed more than 10,000 open-heart operations, including more than 850 heart transplants and over 350 implantations of artificial hearts.

In 2001 Copeland, along with two colleagues, formed SynCardia Systems, Inc. to take over ownership of artificial heart technology from the UA. The company is prospering today and experiencing record implants of artificial hearts.

Copeland left UA in 2010 to "try new things that would benefit patients" at UCSD Cardiovascular Center and Children's Hospital in San Diego.

Andrew Weil (1942-) was born in Philadelphia, received an A.B. degree in botany from Harvard in 1964 and an M.D. from Harvard Medical School in 1968, completed a medical internship at Mt. Zion Hospital in San Francisco, and worked a year with the National Institute of Mental Health. Then, as a Fellow of the Institute of Current World Affairs, Weil traveled widely in North and South America and Africa, collecting information on drug use in other cultures, medicinal plants, and alternative methods of treating disease. From 1971-84 he was on the research staff of the Harvard Botanical Museum and conducted investigations of medicinal and psychoactive plants.

In 1994 Weil founded the Arizona Center for Integrative Medicine at UA's Health Sciences Center where he continues as Director today. Weil espouses the combination of traditional medicine with alternative therapies such as omega-3 fatty acids, vitamin D, herbal remedies, meditation and other "spiritual" strategies. Nutrition, exercise, and stress reduction are emphasized. The Center is training doctors and nurse practitioners in this body-mind-spirit philosophy.

Weil has become an internationally-recognized expert for his views on leading a healthy lifestyle, his philosophy of healthy aging, and his critique of the future of medicine and healthcare. He has written 11 books, with sales of approximately 10 million copies.

Sports

Tucson's movers and shakers in sports include the dean of UA coaches and sports administrators, and UA coaches for basketball, swimming and softball. **James Fred "Pop" McKale** was athletic director of UA from 1915-1957 and coached football, basketball, and baseball. **Lute Olson** was head coach of UA basketball for 25 years and led Arizona to four NCAA Final Four appearances and a National Championship in 1997. UA swim coach **Frank Busch**'s swimmers won 49 NCAA individual titles, 31 NCAA relay titles, and both the men's and women's NCAA team championships in 2008. **Mike Candrea**, as UA women's softball coach, has led his teams to eight NCAA Women's College World Series titles.

James Fred McKale (1887-1967) was born in Lansing, Michigan, graduated from high school there, earned a B.A. degree in chemistry and history at Albion College in 1910, taught history and coached at Tucson High from 1911 to 1914, "when by popular acclaim," he joined the UA faculty.

McKale was appointed Athletic Director in 1915, and according to the Pima County Sports hall of fame, "He coached every major sport and made Arizona's athletic program the finest in the Southwest, leading teams in football for 17 years and in baseball for 35 years."

Tradition says that McKale is responsible for UA's long-standing nickname and its most recognizable slogan. In 1914, after a particularly hard-fought football game, McKale began to call his

"Pop" McKale served as UA Athletic Director for 35 years. (Courtesy of amazon.com)

teams "wildcats." And in 1926, a star football player's dying words to coach McKale following an automobile accident were supposedly, "tell the team to bear down."

McKale acquired a nickname himself when former students and athletes stopped by following their return from World War II to chat with "Pop" McKale.

The UA campus honors "The Grand Old Man of Arizona Sports" with two buildings, Bear Down Gym and the McKale Center, UA's home basketball venue.

Lute Olson (1934-) was born Robert Luther Olson in Mayville, North Dakota to Norwegian-American parents, attended high school in Grand Forks where he led his team to the state basketball championship, attended Augsburg College in Minnesota where he was a three-sport athlete, coached high school basketball in Minnesota and California, then Long Beach City Junior College, followed by a year at Long Beach State and nine years at the University of Iowa, before coming to UA in 1973.

Lute Olson is considered one of the best coaches in college basketball history. (Courtesy of National Basketblog)

Under Olson, Arizona quickly rose to national prominence. In addition to his success in the NCAA basketball tournament, Olson's teams won 11 Pac-10 championships and had 20 consecutive 20-win seasons. Olson was named Pac-10 Coach of the Year seven times and National Coach of the Year twice, in 1988 and 1990.

Olson was known for player development; many of his players went on to impressive careers in the NBA. The UA basketball program has been dubbed "Point Guard U" because of numerous players who have excelled at that position, including current assistant coach David Stoudamire.

With his 46 NCAA tournament wins, "Lute Olson is regarded as one of the greatest coaches in the history of college basketball."

Frank Busch (1951-) was born in Edgewood, Kentucky, received a BS in Education from Loyola University in Chicago, coached community programs for six years in northern Kentucky, and coached swimming at the University of Cincinnati for nine years, before coming to UA in 1989.

Busch transformed Arizona swimming and diving into one of the nation's most powerful programs, maintaining a steady presence in the Top 10. He was named Coach of the Year six times by the NCAA, 11 times by the Pac-10, and once each by United States Swimming and the United States Olympic Committee.

He was a coach for the USA Olympic teams in 2004 and 2008.

Frank Busch spent 22 years at UA before leaving to become the National Team Director of USA Swimming in 2011.

Mike Candrea (1955-) was born in New Orleans, Louisiana, earned an Associate degree at Central Arizona College (CAC) in 1975, a Bachelor's degree at Arizona State in 1978, and a Master's degree from ASU in 1980. Candrea began his softball coaching career at CAC from 1981-1985, where his teams won the national junior college world series his last two years, before coming to UA in 1986.

Under Candrea, the Arizona women's softball team became one of the top programs in the U.S. and perennial powerhouse in the NCAA. Through 2014 his softball teams have won 1387 NCAA games, along with nine Pac-10 conference titles, and have produced 52 All-Americans and four national players of the year. Candrea has earned 10 Pac-10 Coach of the Year awards.

Candrea also coached the U.S. Olympic softball team to a gold medal in 2004 and a silver medal in 2008.

Mike Candrea starts his 30th year as UA softball coach in 2015.

Chapter 4

How Stagecoaches Helped Tucson Develop

If it weren't for stagecoaches, Tucson wouldn't have developed to be the town we see today!

Stagecoaches are public conveyances that carry mail, express, and/or passengers. The term "stage" originally referred to the distance between stages or stations on a route.

Overland Stagecoach Service through Tucson
1857-1881

In 1850, two years after its gold rush began in 1848, California became the 31st state of the Union, separated from the rest of the country by the vast expanse of the Great Plains and the Rocky Mountains. Mail delivery to California from the East took at least a month and a half by steamship and pack animal across Panama. From the beginning, California pressured the U. S. Government to provide faster mail service.

It took five more years for military expeditions and surveyors to establish a trail across the southwestern U.S. that stagecoaches could use year round for overland mail delivery. Starting in 1846, the military (Cooke, Kearny) had blazed trails across Arizona to bring American troops to California to help in the Mexican War (1846-1848). Thousands of gold seekers crossed Arizona in the late 1840s and early 1850s on their way to the California gold fields. Finally in 1854-55 Lieutenant John G. Parke surveyed a potential transcontinental railroad route across southern Arizona that would become the basic route for the first overland mail.

In terms of today's place names, the route entered Arizona from Lordsburg, New Mexico, extended west to Tucson, northwest to the Sacaton area before turning west to the Gila River and on to Yuma and exiting Arizona - generally following the path of today's Interstate 10 and Interstate 8.

Tucson had only been an American town since becoming part of the New Mexico Territory with the Gadsden Purchase from Mexico, approved by Congress on June 29, 1854. As described by historian C. L. Sonnichsen, Tucson in the late 1850s "was still a Mexican village," with a population of a few hundred people, and few Americans.

In July 1857 the San Antonio & San Diego Mail Line began twice-a-month stagecoach runs over the new overland route, carrying both mail and passengers. However, the operation lasted less than a year - because of the death of the company's founder and increasing competition.

Butterfield Overland Mail

In late 1857 John Butterfield of Utica, New York won a government contract for the unheard of sum of $600,000 (over $16.5 million in 2013) per year for six years to carry mail from St. Louis, Missouri to San Francisco, California. The agreement was to provide overland stagecoach service twice a week in each direction; each trip of 2,800 miles was to be completed in 25 days or less. Mail was first priority but passengers were accepted for a total-route cost of $200 ($5,510 in 2013), not including meals.

The Wells Fargo Company, already consolidating small express lines in California, participated with John Butterfield to invest in the Overland Mail. (Wells Fargo would go on to establish an empire in the West - including Arizona, transporting treasure and express by stagecoaches.

The company operated stage lines under its own name in other Western states, but never in Arizona.)

Butterfield spent most of 1858 on the monumental task of constructing and supplying 139 (later about 180) relay stations along the route through what is now Missouri, Arkansas, Oklahoma, Texas, New Mexico, Arizona and California. There was a secondary spur route to Memphis Tennessee on the eastern end of the overland trail, departing from the principal route at Fort Smith, Arkansas.

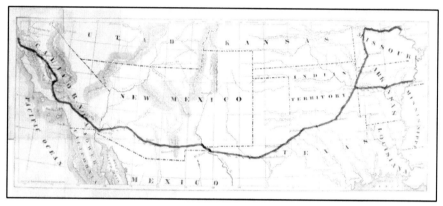

The government-proposed Butterfield Overland Mail route extended from Saint Louis and Memphis in the East to San Francisco in the West. Butterfield modified the route in many places - one example is that after leaving Arizona heading westward, it turned south into northern Mexico before turning north and returning to California. (Courtesy of Wikimedia Commons)

The stage stops at intervals of 9-60 miles (average 20) were places where the coaches could change drivers and draft animals, and the passengers could get water and food. Most stations were simple adobe structures with attached corrals for the animals pulling the coaches. There were ten stone-fortified stations where there was expected to be some trouble with Indians. The coaches traveled at breakneck speeds night and day, regardless of weather and road conditions, except for brief stops at the way stations.

At its peak, Butterfield's Overland Mail employed about 800 people and ran around 100 coaches with 1,000 horses and 500 mules.

Two types of stagecoaches were used on the Butterfield Trail: large, high-quality Concord stagecoaches and much smaller Celerity stage wagons.

Concord stagecoaches were built in Concord, New Hampshire, weighed about 2,500 pounds and were suspended on thick, six-or-eight-ply leather belts called "thoroughbraces" to insulate them from the constant pounding of the wheels over makeshift roads. The Concord coaches could accommodate up to nine passengers inside the coach, with additional room on top for the hearty.

John Butterfield designed the Celerity stage wagon for the portions of the route where the trail was not well developed (like the southwestern desert) - in sand, and for traversing steep inclines. As stagecoach historian Gerald T. Ahnert describes, "It was basically an open buckboard. ... A wooden bench seat was at the front for the driver and conductor. Behind them were three more wooden bench seats for passengers. Wooden staves held up a thin canvas top." About 66 of these stage (Celerity) wagons were built.

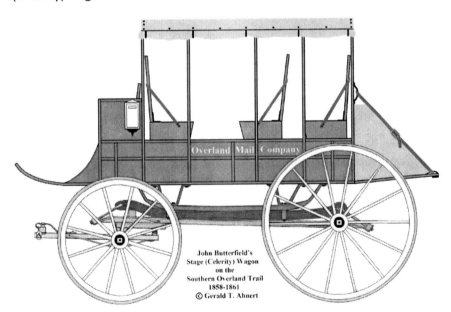

John Butterfield's
Stage (Celerity) Wagon
on the
Southern Overland Trail
1858-1861
© Gerald T. Ahnert

The celerity stage wagon, weighing about one half as much as a Concord stagecoach, was the only type of stagecoach used in Arizona by the Butterfield Overland Mail Company. (Courtesy of Gerald T. Ahnert)

Of the two types of stagecoaches, only the Celerity stage wagon was used in Arizona by Butterfield's Overland Mail Company.

The wagons were pulled by a team of 4-6 horses or mules, many wild and unbroken. Mules provided extra "toughness" for long, hot stretches, particularly in the Arizona desert.

Comfort was not a priority. More than three weeks of constant pounding on the rough route, to say nothing of lack of water and hostile Indians, made for a physically and mentally exhausting trip.

Raphael Pumpelly, a mining engineer heading to silver mines in southern Arizona in 1860, described his overland trip:

> "The coach was fitted with three seats, and these were occupied by nine passengers. As the occupants of the front and middle seats faced each other, it was necessary for these six people to interlock their knees; and there being room inside for only ten of the twelve legs, each side of the coach was graced by a foot, now dangling near the wheel, now trying in vain to find a place of support. ... The fatigue of uninterrupted traveling by day and night in a crowded coach, and the most uncomfortable positions, was beginning to tell seriously upon all the passengers, and was producing a condition bordering on insanity."

Across Arizona

The overland route across Arizona's dry and sparsely populated desert landscape was 437 miles long with 27 stagecoach stations. (Note: Historian Ahnert talks of 25 or 26 stations, pointing out that the Yuma station was really just west across the Colorado River in California and that the Filibuster Stage Station was dropped in the middle of 1859).

It took about four days to get through Arizona at an average speed of about four and a half miles an hour.

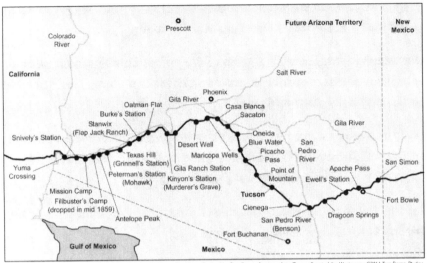

The Butterfield Overland Mail route across Arizona was 437 miles long.

The first eastbound Butterfield Overland Mail stagecoach reached Tucson from San Francisco on September 23, 1858. The first westbound coach from St. Louis reached Tucson on October 2nd. Thereafter westbound mail was due at 1:30 pm on Tuesdays and Fridays; the eastbound at 3:00 am on Wednesdays and Saturdays.

The Buckley House (formerly the Santa Cruz residence) was turned into Tucson's stage station with Sam Hughes (later prominent in the incorporation of the City of Tucson and establishment of public education) hired as the first station agent. The station's location in modern day Tucson was approximately one block north of the State of Arizona complex at Congress Street and Main Avenue.

Wells Fargo established an office in Tucson in 1860, as a convenient mid-point for both east-west and north-south (to Mexico) traffic. William S. Oury, later to be Tucson's first mayor, was selected as agent.

Stagecoaches traveling to California from Tucson headed directly north up Main Street, then northwest along the Santa Cruz River to a stop at Point of Mountain (sometimes called Pointer Mountain) about 18 miles from Tucson. The Point of Mountain station, named for the prominent peak at the northern end of the Tucson Mountains, was located in today's greater Marana, near the West Avra Valley Road exit (242) from Interstate 10. Westbound stages continued northwest to stations near Picacho Peak and Eloy.

Eastbound stages from Tucson headed southeast out of town, crossed present day Davis Monthan Air Force Base, and continued southeast on a path a little north of today's Interstate 10 to a stage station at Cienega, about 35 miles from Tucson. Cienega means "marshy place" and the station provided plenty of trees and water. The station's location was on Cienega Creek, in today's Vail area, off the Marsh Station exit (281) from Interstate 10, about four miles northeast, at the railroad tracks. Coaches continuing to the east headed to the next stations near today's Benson and then Dragoon Springs.

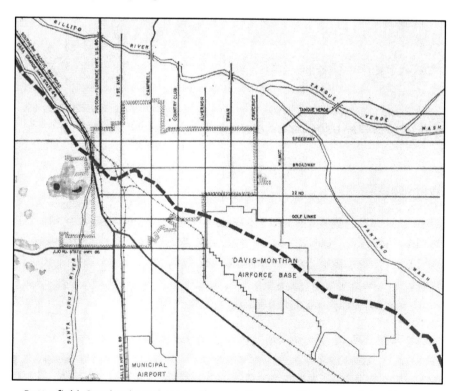

Butterfield Overland Mail route through Tucson. (Courtesy of the Western Postal History Library)

Butterfield Overland Mail operations continued through Tucson until the spring of 1861, when the threat of Civil War and Texas's seceding from the Union forced the southern transcontinental stage line to move north, following a central overland route through the future states of Nebraska, Wyoming, Utah, and Nevada.

Sketch of Butterfield's Celerity stage wagon approaching Tucson, October 1858, by William Hayes Hilton. (Courtesy of Huntington Library)

Other Providers

During the Civil War (1861-1865) Arizona had to rely on military couriers for mail service. But, by 1866 mail and people were again arriving in Tucson - this time from Prescott on Arizona Stagecoach Company coaches. There were connections in Prescott - both west and east - along more northern east-west routes through Arizona.

Meanwhile far to the north, starting in April 1860, the Pony Express crossed the western U.S. to Sacramento, California - ending operations when the overland telegraph was completed in October 1861. Eight years later in 1869 the first transcontinental railroad (to San Francisco) was completed at Promontory Summit Utah, ending stagecoach service on the central overland trail.

Part of Butterfield's southern overland stagecoach route was reactivated in 1870 when the Tucson, Arizona City [Yuma] & San Diego Stage Company started tri-weekly service. Connections to the east were offered in 1872 by the J. F. Bennett & Company. In the mid-to-late 1870s overland stagecoach services between California and the east through Tucson were offered by three companies: Southern Pacific Mail Line, Texas and California Stage Line, and the National Mail & Transportation Company.

Tucson was already becoming in Sonnichsen's words, "an increasingly important commercial center" when the eastern-proceeding southern route of the transcontinental railroad reached Tucson from California in 1880. Tucson's population had grown to about 7,000. Prospectors and ranchers had begun exploring north and south and established new settlements.

Overland stagecoach operations through Tucson ended with the completion of the transcontinental railroad in Texas in 1881, but stagecoach services connecting Arizona settlements, and from Tucson to mining, business, and commerce centers were just beginning and would continue for the next 40 years.

As of January 2015 the National Park Service (NPS), in response to a Congressional mandate, was drafting a feasibility study for a Butterfield National Historic Trail. When the draft is completed, the study will go out for public review, then to the Secretary of the Interior who will submit it to Congress for approval.

The primary rationale for the NPS action towards a National Trail is "that it fulfilled a critical need: to tie California and other western territories more closely to the long-established portions of the U.S. east of the Mississippi River. In addition, the Butterfield Mail was a major public development. It was the first thread of civilization in an otherwise desolate, isolated world."

A Half Century of Tucson-Area Stagecoach Service
1870- 1920s

The first non-native miners in southern Arizona were Spaniards who began drifting north from long-established mining areas in today's Sonora, Mexico in the 1730s. Mexicans continued prospecting in the borderland country following their independence from Spain in 1821. Immediately after the Gadsden Purchase in 1854, when the borderlands became the property of the U.S., Americans began exploring these same mining areas, rediscovering some of the old Spanish and Mexican diggings.

When the first Butterfield overland stagecoach reached Tucson in 1858, Americans had already established silver mines near Arivaca and in the Santa Rita and Patagonia Mountains.

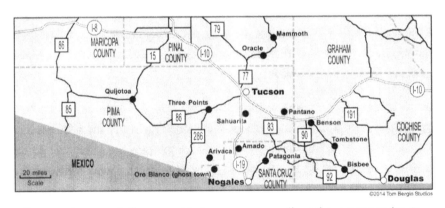

Tucson stagecoach lines provided passenger, mail, and express service to southern Arizona mining towns. (Courtesy of Tom Bergin)

Stagecoaches South

While American mining was developing, in 1870 experienced freighter Pedro Aguirre started the Arizona & Sonora Stage Line in Tucson to carry mail and passengers between Tucson and Altar, Sonora Mexico, with connections southward to the Sonoran capital Hermosillo and the important Gulf of California port at Guaymas.

In 1873 gold was discovered south of Arivaca, near the border with Mexico, setting off an American mining boom and the development of the Oro Blanco mining camp. This strike, along with successful silver mining around Arivaca, led Pedro Aguirre in 1877 to start regular stagecoach service to Arivaca, south to Oro Blanco, with continuing service to Altar, Sonora.

Aguirre continued to provide stagecoach service to this intermittently successful borderland mining region until 1886 when he sold his company and retired to his Buenos Ayres ranch west of Arivaca.

From 1892-1908 stagecoach service to Arivaca and Oro Blanco was provided by Mariano Samaniego, a Sonoran-born freighter, cattle rancher, merchant, and the acknowledged most successful Hispanic Tucson public official in Arizona's territorial period.

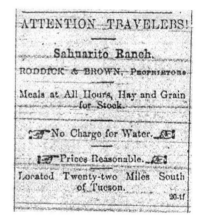

Stagecoaches heading south from Tucson stopped at James Brown's Sahuarita Ranch and the "halfway" station in Amado to change horses or mules and obtain food for passengers. The stop in Amado was also known as the "junction" because the route to Arivaca branched west from there.

This newspaper ad for a stage stop ran in the Arizona Daily Star in January 1878.

Stagecoaches Southeast

Two of Arizona's biggest mining strikes occurred in southeastern Arizona in 1877. Discovery of huge deposits of silver and copper led to the development of Tombstone in 1879 and Bisbee in 1880.

Within a month of arriving in Tucson from Kansas in October 1878, J. D. Kinnear started Kinnear's Express stagecoach service (every four days) to the new silver area. By 1879 Kinnear had formed the Tucson & Tombstone Stage Line to provide daily service to Tombstone and soon thereafter on to Bisbee. In the spirited competition to provide the best service, another new Tombstone arrival from Kansas, named Wyatt Earp, sold out his own stagecoach line interests to Kinnear.

Stages from Tucson to Tombstone and Bisbee started out using the old Butterfield overland stage relay stations at Cienega and San Pedro near Benson. When the southern transcontinental railroad tracks were laid right over the station at Cienega in 1880, a new station was built a mile and half to the east at Pantano. The San Pedro station was "re-opened," advertising "excellent meals for the traveler," in the *Tucson Daily Citizen*.

At about the same time as service to Tombstone and Bisbee was developing, stagecoaches from Tucson via Pantano began routes to mines around Patagonia.

Stagecoaches North

Fifty miles northeast of Tucson, near Mammoth, gold was discovered in 1879. William "Curly" Neal, of African American and Cherokee descent, came to Tucson in 1878, opened a livery and by 1879 was running a stage line to the mining towns around Mammoth, with a stage stop in Oracle. In 1895 Neal financed the building of the luxurious Mountain View Hotel on his ranch in Oracle.

Stagecoaches West

Also in 1879 silver was discovered in Quijotoa, 65 miles west of Tucson, but it wasn't until 1883 that rich croppings generated real excitement. Richard Starr (of Starr Pass fame) pioneered a stagecoach trail through the Tucson Mountains as a quick route to Quijotoa. The stage stop out of Tucson was the ranch house of the Robles Ranch in Three Points. Unfortunately the mining boom in Quijotoa only lasted until 1885, with a consequent drop-off in stage business.

In addition to the mining regions discussed above, Tucson stagecoaches provided service for many years to smaller copper mining areas such as Helvetia, north of Madera Canyon in the Santa Rita Mountains; Mineral Hill, just west of Sahaurita; and Silver Bell, northwest of Tucson.

Stagecoach Network

While stagecoach service to southern Arizona mining regions was developing, Tucson remained a "hub" on an increasing stagecoach transportation network among other settlements in Territorial Arizona, including Nogales, Casa Grande, Florence, Phoenix, Prescott, and Globe.

The stagecoach business was dynamic. Stage companies went out of business or changed names frequently. As improved roads replaced rough wagon trails, the coaches themselves changed to smaller, lighter stages, wagons, or buckboards. The vehicles were pulled by teams of two, four, or six horses or mules.

A survey of stage line records and advertisements in Tucson newspapers between 1880 and 1910 shows that stagecoach service to destinations within 75 miles of Tucson was provided several times a week, sometimes daily, and completed in one day. Fares for passengers remained relatively constant over the period at approximately ten cents per mile, decreasing slightly over the longer routes. During that entire period I could have traveled 65 miles from Tucson to Arivaca (as my grandparents did in 1905) for six dollars.

Not all stagecoach trips were "rides in the park." Here is what Ines Fraser, on the way to the mines south of Arivaca to join her husband in 1904, said about her stagecoach trip in a letter to her granddaughter:

> "We were underway! The mountains were beautiful; the road for several miles was good, though unworked, for it was on firm, slightly sandy ground. ... When we reached the 'Junction,' a stage rest stop at the turnoff for Arivaca and the borderland mining country, it had just stopped raining and everything looked cool and clean.

"The miles from the Junction to Arivaca were over rolling country, with good 'natural' roads – but not good at the arroyo crossings. Our stagecoach had to wait on the brink of a steep-sided, narrow-bottom arroyo till the rush of water from a flash flood quieted down and decreased until the stage team could safely descend and scramble like fury up the opposite bank, slippery after the rain. The driver had to know his business and Arizona 'flash floods' and how to urge his horses up the steep other side. No one but an experienced teamster ... and strong, obedient horses, used to the roads, could possibly have taken heavy loads up and down those arroyo crossings during the rainy season."

My grandfather Eugene Ring and grandmother Grace Ring are seated in the rear seat of this stagecoach in front of the way station in Arivaca in 1905. (Courtesy of the Ring family)

Transporting Valuables

In 1877, in response to increased mining activity in southern Arizona, Wells-Fargo Express Company, transporter of valuables, reestablished its Tucson office that had been briefly operational in 1860 for the Butterfield Overland Mail. Wells Fargo began leasing space on stagecoaches to carry "treasure boxes," a good source of income for stage lines, but somewhat risky.

According to the fascinating book, *Encyclopedia of Stage Robbery in Arizona*, there were 129 stagecoach robberies in Arizona between 1875 and 1903. Eleven of these occurred in Pima County, including two robberies near present day Marana, single robberies near Patagonia and present day Green Valley, and a robbery of the Tucson-Quijotoa stage. The Marana robbery in 1878 was committed by highwayman Bill Brazelton, who supposedly turned his horse's shoes around to confuse trackers, but was later shot dead by a pursuing posse.

End of an Era

With increased links to population centers and agriculture, livestock, and mining enterprises, Tucson's population grew to about 14,000 people by 1910. Stagecoach lines were prosperous right up the time of Arizona statehood in 1912. But by that time, local railroads, e.g., Tucson to Nogales, had proliferated, and automobiles and trucks began to take the place of horse or mule driven stagecoaches.

A few local Tucson mail contract stagecoach services continued into the 1920s. One of these was mail delivery from 1914-1921 between Tucson and Wrightstown Ranch at the corner of Harrison and Wrightstown Roads.

Today, more than 100 years after statehood, if you "Google" "Tucson Stagecoach" you get a long list of van shuttle services that you can use to get to the Tucson International Airport or to Phoenix. Sadly, the romantic age of the stagecoach is over, but it's nice to know that "stagecoaches," so important to Tucson's development, are still operating today!

If you want to see what a real Concord stagecoach from the 1860s was like, you can see one at Tucson's Arizona Historical Society Museum.

Chapter 5

Historic Rillito River Communities

Around 1900 two communities developed along Tucson's Rillito River - communities that flourished because of plentiful and dependable River water. One of these was a pioneer Mormon settlement that included farms just north of the River bend and the more urban settlement of Binghampton (pronounced bing-hámp-ton), south of the Rillito River at today's North Dodge Boulevard and East Fort Lowell Road. The second community, old Fort Lowell, east of the Mormons, was started by Mexican farmers and ranchers.

The underlying geological structure of these near-River areas holds ground water closer to the surface than in other parts of the Tucson basin. That, plus the convergence of the Tanque Verde and Pantano desert waterways to form the Rillito (where the present day Craycroft Bridge crosses the River) provided a reliable water supply for centuries. (Extensive human use of surface water, and groundwater pumping that started in earnest in the 1940s, have lowered the water table and now keep the creeks, washes, and rivers dry most of the year.)

The first settlers along this section of the Rillito were Native American Hohokam. Archaeological evidence suggests that between 450–1450 AD the Hohokam built houses, dug canals to water their fields, fashioned pottery, and raised their families.

Other than a few Mexican and Anglo settlers starting in the 1850s, the next residents along the eastern Rillito came in 1873, when the U.S Army built Fort Lowell to protect citizens against Apache attacks. The Army occupied Fort Lowell until 1891.

Mormon Binghampton

In 1899 Nephi Bingham, a Mormon, started working a small farm just north of the River bend. In 1904 Nephi and his family moved south of the River to a location that quickly became known as Bingham's place. At the time, there was only one house between their home and Tucson, six miles away by wagon road.

A little farming community of Bingham relatives began to grow on both sides of the River. Seeking to escape political unrest and revolution in Mexico, Mormons started coming north in 1909 from a colony in Colonia Dublan to join Nephi. (Republican presidential candidate Mitt Romney's father was born there in 1907.) Additional Mormons from Safford, Thatcher, Duncan, Pima, St. David, Douglas, and Benson joined the community which soon became known as Binghampton.

Plentiful Water

The settlement thrived - based on plentiful water. Nephi hired Yaqui Indians to dig a ditch to draw water from Tanque Verde Creek two miles to the east, near old Fort Lowell. A strong underground flow there provided unfailing water.

According to Duane Bingham, whose grandfather was the younger brother of Bingham family patriarch Nephi Bingham, the Rillito used to have very shallow banks, the current steep banks resulting from dredging by mining operations over the years. He describes a digging tool called a "Fresno Scraper," a sort of open-front-end, horse-drawn wheelbarrow that was used to help dig the irrigation ditches.

They stored the water in two large ponds near present day North Alvernon Way, just south of the River, and irrigated their farmland from the Rillito, the reservoirs, and shallow wells.

They planted vegetable gardens and orchards, and ran dairies.

Water from Tanque Verde Creek was drawn via an irrigation ditch to Binghampton storage ponds, large enough for boats. (Courtesy of Duane Bingham, circa 1920s)

Constructing a Church

In 1910 the Binghampton Branch of the Mormon Church was organized. Worshipers built a frame/adobe school south of the River - where children learned during the week, and everyone attended church on Sunday. In 1927 members began constructing the church building that was dedicated in 1935, remodeled extensively since, and is still operating today at 3750 East Fort Lowell Road.

The Church was the center of activity for the Binghampton settlement which would eventually grow to an area bounded by North Country Club

Road and North Swan Road to the west and east, East Fort Lowell Road to the south, and the base of the foothills on the north.

This Mormon Church at 3750 East Fort Lowell Road was dedicated in 1935 by Binghampton residents. (Courtesy of Bob Ring)

Also existing today is the Binghampton Cemetery, north of the Rillito, at 4001 North Alvernon Way, almost hidden in the beautiful foothills desert. The 40-acre cemetery dates back to 1899, is now managed by Duane Bingham, accommodates over 1500 interments, and is still accepting burials.

Gradual Decline

The population of Binghampton probably exceeded 300 people by the early 1920s. Farming continued to thrive until the 1930s when reduced Rillito River flow, declining water tables, and the Great Depression forced residents to find other jobs.

From the late 1920s through the 1930s, Binghampton experienced an influx of non-Mormon ranchers and farmers who established horse-riding schools, boarding stables, horse ranches, and pecan groves in place of the family farms. The community remained mostly agrarian until the early 1950s.

By the 1960s many Binghampton residents had moved farther out of town to the suburbs. The area was rezoned for multiple-use, drastically changing the character of the neighborhood.

Today, a drive through the old Binghampton community reveals mostly a collection of small businesses, only a few original (but heavily modified) homes, and no signposts relating the community's fascinating history.

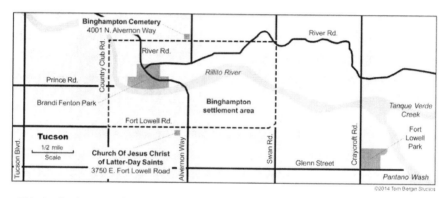

This is the layout of the Mormon Binghampton community that dates from 1899. (Courtesy of Tom Bergin)

Remembering Binghampton

More positively, in 2003 the 427-acre Binghampton Rural Historic Landscape was designated to save what was left of the rural area, just north of the River, approximately at North Dodge Boulevard and East River Road.

In 2006 Brandi Fenton Memorial Park, 56 acres within the Binghampton Rural Historic Landscape, was dedicated as part of the Pima County parks system. Tucson's Fenton family initiated a unique public-private partnership to help fund and develop the park in memory of their daughter who was killed in an auto accident in 2003 when she was just 13. The park provides a number of very well done Binghampton-history exposition signs along its pleasant sidewalks. Access to the park is from the rerouted North Alvernon Way near its intersection with East River Road and also via Tucson's popular river walk and bike paths.

Old Fort Lowell

When the US Army started development of Fort Lowell in the early 1870s, where Tanque Verde and Pantano Creeks joined to form the Rillito River, the streams flowed freely most of the year. A dense mesquite forest grew there and the desert oasis contained many birds, mammals, and plants - some unknown before then.

The soldiers found remains of prehistoric Hohokam habitation and a couple of irrigation ditches, probably dug in the 1860s by Mexican and Anglo settlers, to draw water from the Tanque Verde to their farms to the west of Fort Lowell (as the Mormons in Binghampton would do 40 years later).

Both the Army and nearby settlers exploited the then-plentiful water, but argued constantly over land and water rights, and use of the canals. The Fort relied on water from shallow wells and water diverted from the pre-existing irrigation ditches.

Fort Lowell grew to include about 30 adobe buildings with barracks, a hospital, commissary, stables, trading store, guard house, kitchens, a large parade ground, and tree-lined sidewalks. Additional wooden structures, barracks, sheds, and equipment buildings were constructed in the mid-1880s when the Fort was at peak occupation of more than 250 officers and soldiers.

After the Army abandoned Fort Lowell in 1891 - with the threat from the Apache eliminated, the Department of the Interior sold the Fort's lumber, tin roofing, doors, and windows. The adobe buildings began to disintegrate from weathering and vandalism.

Mexican Settlers Arrive

But Mexican immigrants searching for a better life, and attracted by the relative abundance of water, began to arrive. They replaced doors, windows, and roofs and lived within the old adobe walls, raising families and livestock. The men cut wood for their needs and took some to

This is Fort Lowell's Officers Row Lane as it appeared in 1888. (Courtesy of Arizona Historical Society, 42674)

Tucson for sale. They made adobes, worked in construction, and raised gardens. The women did the washing in the irrigation ditches. The place came to be known as El Fuerte (the Fort).

In the 1920s and 1930s the Mexican families who had settled in the Fort began to find lots west along East Fort Lowell Road and to build small adobe "Sonora Ranch" style houses. They dug wells, finding water at less than 30 feet depth. They built a school and a succession of small churches, dedicating the San Pedro Chapel in 1932. By the late 1940s the little community of perhaps 300 people had added a store and a cemetery, and become a social center for people in the broader area.

Anglos were also attracted to the neighborhood. In 1900 three of the abandoned Fort's officers quarters and their kitchens were purchased for use as a sanatorium. In 1928 the Adkins family bought part of the old Fort land (including the sanatorium) at the southwest corner of North Craycroft Road and East Fort Lowell Road and began the business that became the Adkins Steel Manufacturing Company. By the late 1930s there were several Anglo families living in the community, including a well-driller and prominent farmers.

Transition to Anglo Community

By the mid-1940s the land was bare except for a few mesquite trees. Most trees had been cut for firewood, building, or farming. Wells were going dry as the water table lowered steadily due to greater Tucson's pumping of underground water.

In 1948 St. Cyril of Alexandria Catholic Church was built on North Swan Road at East Pima Street. The little chapel of San Pedro was abandoned and used as a private residence.

The old Fort Lowell neighborhood was gradually transitioning from a Mexican American community to an Anglo community.

By the 1960s Glenn Aire subdivision had been built west of the old Fort and North Craycroft Road was extended north from East Fort Lowell Road, first to the River in 1929, and later to cross the Rillito River. The extension in 1929 demolished one of the old Fort's officers quarters and cut the Fort grounds in half.

Starting in the 1950s there were several efforts to turn old Fort Lowell into a recreational park. By the 1970s the area had become a Pima County Park, with swimming pool, and playing fields.

Preserving Fort Lowell

Over the years there were also many efforts to try to understand Fort Lowell's historic past and preserve some of its buildings. Archaeological studies of Hohokam sites began in 1935. Pima County and even the Boy Scouts of America were active in sporadic restoration activities of Fort Lowell ruins from the 1940s to the 1960s. The Fort Museum was opened in 1963, administered by the Arizona Historical Society. Fort Lowell was placed on the National Register of Historic Places in 1978, while the formation of the Fort Lowell Historic District was completed in 1981.

The reconstructed Officers Quarters serves as the museum for Fort Lowell Park. (Courtesy of Bob Ring)

Also in 1981 the Old Fort Lowell Neighborhood Association was formed to help plan for the preservation of the larger Fort Lowell community.

The old San Pedro Chapel became the first City of Tucson Landmark in 1982, and was subsequently placed on both the State and National Register of Historic Places. With assistance from an Arizona Heritage Foundation grant, private donations, and fund raising activities, in 1993 the Old Fort Lowell Neighborhood Association purchased the Chapel and started efforts to preserve the building and restore its original character.

With Tucson continually expanding, Fort Lowell Park was transferred to the City of Tucson in 1984. Since then, the development and historic preservation of the Park has been guided by a periodically updated Master Plan.

The Old Fort Lowell Neighborhood Association continues today to plan the development of the community of roughly one square mile, bounded by the Rillito River on the north, East Glenn Street on the south, North Swan Road on the west, and Pantano Wash on the east.

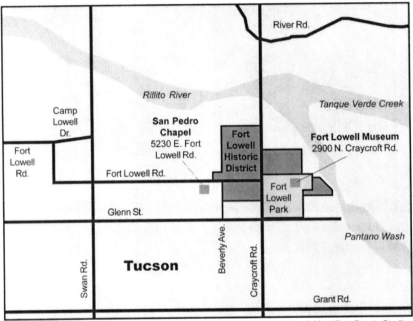

Old Fort Lowell survives today in the form of an historic neighborhood district and a city park. (Courtesy of Tom Bergin)

The Association hosts an annual Fort Lowell Day Celebration that features walking tours, cavalry drills, vintage baseball games, music, food, and youth activities.

A drive through the neighborhood today clearly shows a proud sense of community and appreciation for its history.

Chapter 6

Watch Tucson Grow to the Northeast

What follows is a whimsical time-travel inspired review of Tucson's growth to the northeast and the development of two of Tucson's more affluent communities. Subjects covered include: The Beginnings, Exploration and Initial Settlement, Access to Natural Recreation Areas, Development of the Catalina Foothills, and Development of the Tanque Verde Valley.

The Beginnings

Imagine that you are in a time machine, sitting in La Encantada shopping mall's parking lot, right in front of AJ's. You look out to see the beautiful Santa Catalina Mountains. Now you push a button and travel back in time twelve million years. Surprise, the Santa Catalina Mountains don't exist!

Formative Years *12 Million Years Ago*

At this point in time you see only a range of small hills. Over the next seven million years or so, as your time machine steadily moves forward in time, the western North American continent stretches and the earth's crust cracks and breaks into huge blocks, bordered by deep faults. Some of the blocks rise and become mountains; others sink, forming valleys. Then comes the artistic part. Over millions of years, wind and streams from melting ice and rainwater erode the landscape. As you remember from the present time, what results are the mostly *granite* Santa Catalina Mountains covering 200 square miles with a peak altitude of 9,157 feet above sea level. Sabino Creek flows south out of the mountains. The Tanque Verde Valley lies in the northeastern corner of the Tucson basin at about 2,400 feet elevation, with two streams, Tanque Verde Creek and Agua Caliente Creek, flowing westward out of the mountains.

It took 12 million years to form the Santa Catalina Mountains that we know today - one of the most beautiful and ecologically diverse regions in the U.S. (Courtesy of Bob Ring)

About 11,000 years ago, near the end of the last ice age, you might spot your first human beings, hunter-gathers from the Clovis culture, hunting ice-age mammoths. As the ice recedes, you notice large bison, deer and other animals.

For the next 10,000 years you observe climate changes that alternate between wet and dry, causing the Sonoran desert and Santa Catalina Mountain forests to retreat and advance correspondingly. Finally, the familiar forested Santa Catalina Mountains and lush high-desert Tanque Verde Valley are spread out before you - one of the most ecologically diverse regions in the U.S.

Native Americans *AD 500*

From about AD 450 to 1450, you watch Hohokam farmers and traders living in villages along the Santa Cruz River in the distance to the southwest. The Hohokam have summer camps in the foothills and mountain canyons to escape the desert high temperatures and to access water in dry periods when the Santa Cruz River flow is interrupted. Over a relatively short period of time, the Hohokam disappear, to be replaced by the Tohono O'odham and Pima, also desert peoples and riverside farmers.

In the early 1600s you will begin to see Apaches, nomadic people who use the Santa Catalinas for hunting and camping. They also collect acorn and piñon nuts and raise small crops of beans, squash, and corn. In a few years, the Apache will also use the mountains as a base to raid enemies to the south.

Spanish and Mexican Influence *1500*

From your time machine vantage point, in the 1500s you might see the first Europeans to visit Arizona. In 1540, barely 20 years after Spanish conqueror Hernando Cortez overthrows the Aztec empire and claims Mexico for Spain, Francisco Vàzquez de Coronado passes through the lower San Pedro River Valley, 40 miles east of Tucson, heading north in search of the rumored Seven Cities of Gold.

In the 1690s you see Father Eusebio Kino visiting the Native American villages along the Santa Cruz River, establishing missions, and beginning the spread of Spanish influence and culture in Arizona. History speculates that Father Kino is the first European to take official note of the Santa Catalina Mountains, supposedly naming them the Santa Caterinas, after either his sister or a desert village of the same name.

You can't see it, but in 1736 there is a big silver discovery, just south of the present border with Mexico. This "Planchas de Plata" strike attracts thousands of Spaniards. After the silver is exhausted, some of these prospectors drift north along the Santa Cruz River, looking for gold or silver in Arizona. Others establish ranches or farms along the Santa Cruz. Their numbers increase rapidly.

You watch the Apache leaving the sanctuaries of their mountain camps to raid the settlements along the Santa Cruz River. In 1775 you see Tucson established as a Spanish presidio, or fort, to protect settlers from the warlike Apache. The Old Pueblo is born.

You see the Mexican flag raised over Tucson in 1821 when Mexico achieves its independence from Spain. Little else changes for 20 years. You do notice that mountain men and trappers from the United States are beginning to explore the mountains, foothills and streams around Tucson.

American Tucson *1849*

Increased activity in Tucson catches your attention in 1849 as wagon trains from the eastern U.S. begin to travel west through southern Arizona on their way to the California Gold Rush. A few years later in 1854, with the Gadsden Purchase, the U.S. buys southern Arizona from Mexico to secure lands for a transcontinental railroad.

You notice that the Civil War, starting in 1861, pretty much brings business to a halt in Tucson. In 1862 Confederate troops occupy Tucson for a couple of months. In 1863 the U.S. Congress approves organization of the Territory of Arizona; Tucson is now officially part of the U.S. You recall that Arizona statehood will not come until 1912.

After the Civil War, Tucson becomes a "destination city" for easterners looking for new lands and opportunities. Tucson begins the transition from a Mexican village to an American city. Stagecoaches transport people and mail around southern Arizona, and connect Tucson with the rest of the country. You watch as Tucson grows rapidly with frontier Americans, and becomes a center for mining and ranching.

Exploration and Initial Settlement

Ranches and Homesteads *1868*

In the late 1850s you watched people beginning to reach out from Tucson toward the north and east to make their living on the open lands of the foothills and valleys. You saw the Tanque Verde Valley (named for large water holes containing green algae) settled by Mexicans, Anglos, and Chinese who started farms and cattle ranches. At the same time you noted a ranch on Sabino Creek, just a mile south of Sabino Canyon. In 1868 well-known Tucson land holder and cattleman, Emilio Carrillo, founds the Tanque Verde Ranch, along Tanque Verde Creek at the far eastern end of the valley. Settlers establish Agua Caliente Ranch at the spring, along Agua Caliente Creek, in 1875.

You can see that these major creeks flow year round. Grasslands are plentiful. A large mesquite forest covers the southeastern Tanque Verde Valley. Cattle roam over expansive areas, even in the foothills. As you will see, these conditions will not last much longer.

In the early 1900s, you will note that William and Maria Watson start developing a 172-acre homestead in the foothills at Pima Canyon. At the same time you will observe a cattle ranch, the Flying V, established at Ventana Canyon.

Between 1890 and 1920 you will see the mesquite forest cut down to provide fuel for residents of the growing city of Tucson. In 1930 Jane Wentworth will build a 640-acre stock-raising homestead on that deforested property. Jane's only neighbors will be thousands of saguaro cacti.

Apache Wars *1873*

In the frontier period, Apaches continue to be a problem. The U.S. Army builds Fort Lowell east of Tucson. From 1873 to 1891, the Army escorts wagon trains, protects settlers, and conducts offensive operations against the Apache. Troopers use Soldier Camp in the Catalinas for intermittent campaigns against the Apache. The Army also establishes a camp at Agua Caliente Spring, part of a protective barrier for Tucson. The Arizona Indian war will end with the final surrender of Geronimo in 1886 and the deportation of remaining Apaches to Florida.

This bronze casting was erected at Fort Lowell Park in 1991 to honor enlisted men who fought in the Apache wars in the 1870s and 1880s. (Courtesy of Bob Ring)

Transcontinental Railroad *1880*

In 1880 you notice a big "hub-bub" in Tucson, the celebration of the arrival of the railroad from California. The transcontinental link will be completed to the east in 1881. The railroad will help increase trade with the rest of the world and bring in heavier equipment for industry, construction, and mining. Trains will also bring in thousands of new permanent residents as well as tourists attracted by the fabulous winter weather and the prospect of a western frontier experience, and people seeking a dry climate to recover from illnesses like tuberculosis.

Two of the first people to arrive in Tucson by train are botanist John Gill Lemmon and his wife Sara Allen Plummer Lemmon - on their honeymoon. In 1880 they climb the Catalinas' highest peak and name it Mount Lemmon in honor of the new bride, who is the first woman to climb the peak.

Mining *1880*

You've noticed prospectors searching for gold and silver in the Santa Catalina Mountains. Starting in the late 1860s, gold seekers worked placer deposits on Cañada del Oro Creek, four to ten miles southwest of the town of Oracle. Prospectors will return to this site time and again for more than a hundred years, but only small amounts of gold will be found.

Mineral seekers will locate a handful of claims on the Tucson side of the mountains, but none will make any money. Gold fever will even strike in Upper Sabino Canyon in 1892, but lasts only briefly as prospectors find little of the precious metal.

Starting in the late 1870s, you've seen most of the mining action occur on the north slope of the Catalinas, on Oracle Ridge. Here miners located and worked several gold and silver claims with some success, but these mines largely become inactive after the mid-1880s. Until the completion of a dirt road from Oracle to the mines (continuing nearly to the top of Mount Lemmon) in 1920, this area will remain largely inaccessible. Prospectors will make sporadic attempts to locate and work new claims over the years, but the only mildly successful activity is copper mining that will last intermittently until 1968.

Guest Ranches and Resorts *1881*

Beginning in the early 1880s, you notice a new phenomenon - guest ranches and resorts. In 1881 Fuller's Hot Springs and Resort opens at Agua Caliente Spring. The next year Sunstone Guest Ranch opens just a few miles to the southwest. Starting in 1908, the Tanque Verde Ranch will invite tourists to participate in roundups, a tradition that continues today.

"Dude" ranches are emerging in the Catalina Foothills. The Flying-V Dude Ranch will evolve from the working cattle ranch in the 1920s. By the 1940s, the large Watson homestead at Pima Canyon will become the Westward Look Resort. In 1948 Hacienda del Sol guest ranch will be born from the previous property, a college preparatory school for young women.

You will see Tucson successfully change its marketing approach from a sanitarium for the sick - to recuperate from arthritis, bronchitis, and tuberculosis - to a tourist attraction for the healthy. Canyon Ranch spa will open in 1979. The ultimate expressions of these tourist attractions will be the foothills' Loews Ventana Canyon Resort & Spa opening in 1984 (with its Flying V Bar and Grill) and the Westin La Paloma Resort opening in 1986. Both of these fabulous resorts will offer championship golf courses to visitors.

Access to Natural Recreation Areas

Sabino Canyon *1885*

By the 1880s Tucsonans are taking to the high country for picnics and to escape the hot weather in the summer. You see lean-to's, campsites, and log cabins begin to appear in the Santa Catalina Mountains. Summer colonies on Mount Lemmon will be evident by 1918 and you will certainly notice the start of the development of Mount Lemmon's Summerhaven community in the 1920s. But lack of a road up Mount Lemmon from the Tucson side, will greatly limit the number of visitors.

Meanwhile, Tucsonans discover Sabino Canyon as a recreation site. You see picnickers on horseback or in horse-drawn carriages or wagons flocking along a rutted dirt road to spend a pleasant day along Sabino Creek in Lower Sabino Canyon. Really adventuresome visitors can reach higher country on narrow horse trails or hiking paths.

How Sabino Canyon got its name will remain a mystery. Possibilities include being named after nearby ranchland, local pioneer Sabino Otero, or since "sabino" is a Spanish word that can be defined as roan or brownish red, the Canyon could have been named after the color of its cliffs or the water in Sabino Creek.

The entrance to spectacular Sabino Canyon is hidden at the center of this landscape. (Courtesy of Bob Ring)

While refreshing mountain recreation resources are being discovered, another resource, water for Tucson's increasing population, begins to become an issue. Already pumping water from the underground aquifer and the Santa Cruz River in the 1880s, Tucsonans wonder about Sabino Creek, flowing out of the Santa Catalina Mountains through Sabino Canyon, as a possible future source of water. Many schemes are proposed, including damming Sabino Creek near the mouth of the canyon.

Before any action is taken on this matter, you notice that in 1887 an earthquake centered in northern Mexico, shakes southern Arizona. You watch huge boulders tumbling down Sabino Canyon's walls into the creek below.

113

Seemingly forgetting this earthquake that so violently affects Sabino Canyon, in 1901 a UA professor proposes a huge dam in the Canyon to create a large reservoir. The dam is to be more than three miles upstream from the mouth of the Canyon, a mile beyond the end of the present road. You see workers start exploratory development. However, much-less-than-predicted water flow rates in Sabino Creek cause this project to collapse in the early 1910s.

The big-dam idea is resurrected during the 1930s depression-era government relief program to turn Sabino Canyon into a recreation area. Having found potable water and electricity sources elsewhere, Tucsonans' objective this time is to attract tourists for boating, fishing, and lake-side camping.

It turns out that no government funds are forthcoming for the dam/lake project so effort concentrates in Lower Sabino Canyon. From 1933 to 1940 you will see work on a road running 3.8 miles into the Canyon - crisscrossing Sabino Creek, nine bridges, campgrounds, and picnic areas. You will notice the small dam built in Lower Sabino Canyon, with a small lake behind for swimming and fishing - enormously popular with Tucson citizens.

Visits to Sabino Canyon will be interrupted by heavy road-closing rains in January 1992 and again in July 2006. You will see that the damage in 2006 is extensive, with some canyon walls crashing down, dumping earth and rock across the road and with runoff water undercutting the roadbed. Many of the small dams on Sabino Creek and picnicking facilities will suffer damage also. But with the help of numerous volunteers, concerned about the future, you will see Sabino Canyon cleaned up and the damaged roads, dams, and facilities restored.

You will see Sabino Canyon closed briefly in March 2004 when several mountain lions are sighted in the Canyon. You will watch with interest as Arizona Game and Fish Department officials track, tranquilize, and relocate two animals and are forced to shoot a third animal.

The Sabino Canyon Recreation Area will continue to very popular for picnicking, hiking, and appreciating the natural environment, becoming one of the biggest tourist attractions in the State of Arizona at 1.5 million visitors per year by 2009.

Catalina Highway *1933*

Also, in 1933 you see the start of construction of the Catalina Highway to Mount Lemmon. This project is also funded by the federal government. The roadway is officially designated the General Hitchcock Highway after Postmaster General Frank Harris Hitchcock, who is primarily responsible for getting the project organized and kicked off.

You see that the early work on the highway is accomplished by prison workers housed in a federal prison camp located at the base of the Santa Catalina Mountains. The road extends north from E. Tanque Verde Road in the Tanque Verde Valley, traverses a winding route up the Catalinas through Summerhaven, intersects near the summit with the dirt road that comes up the north slope of the Santa Catalinas from Oracle, and ends near the top of Mount Lemmon. You will see the twenty-eight mile highway completed in 1950, truly opening up the Santa Catalina Mountains to visitors from Tucson.

The road rises from about 3,000 feet above sea level to approximately 9,100 feet. The scenic drive leaves the saguaro cacti, mesquite trees, and cholla plants of the Sonoran Desert, passes through stands of oak, juniper, and piñon pine, enters pine forests at about 7,000 feet, and then fir and aspen forests on the cooler north-facing slopes above 8,000 feet.

Mount Lemmon Ski Valley will open in 1970 as the southernmost ski resort in the continental U.S.

In 2003 you will watch with horror as the Aspen fire burns for a month on Mount Lemmon, searing 84,750 acres of land, and destroying 340 homes and businesses of the town of Summerhaven.

Forest Service Actions *1933*

While traveling back to the present in your time machine, you've noticed the U.S acting to preserve and improve access to some of the Tucson area's important natural resources. In 1908 the newly created U.S. Forest Service designated the Coronado National Forest that is made up of several elements in southeastern Arizona, including the Santa Catalina Mountains (and Sabino Canyon), the eastern edge of the Tanque Verde Valley, and the Rincon Mountains. In 1933 beautiful stands of saguaro cacti are preserved in the Saguaro National Monument, east and west of Tucson. Both areas will be designated as Saguaro National Park in 1994.

The eastern saguaro monument area defines the southeastern boundary of the Tanque Verde Valley. The federal government attempts to include the privately-owned Jane Wentworth homestead within the monument, but efforts fail, apparently because of the lack of funds during the Great Depression. So this one-square-mile "notch," at the extreme northwest boundary of the monument, is not included.

The Forest Service will construct a road into Lower Bear Canyon in 1960 and build a visitor center for Sabino and Bear Canyons in 1963. A narrated-journey shuttlebus service will begin in 1978 in Sabino Canyon. Also in 1978 the Forest Service will establish the Pusch Ridge Wilderness Area on the southern slope of the Santa Catalinas to provide additional protection for our forests, wildlife, and the natural environment.

Development of the Catalina Foothills

(Time-machine clock: 1933)

First Subdivisions

You noticed that in the late 1920s, Tucson developer John W. Murphey purchased nearly 8,000 acres of federal and state property in the Catalina Foothills.

In 1929 Murphey built an elite college preparatory boarding school for girls, right in the center of the foothills, off today's North Hacienda del Sol Road. A sufficient number of people lived in the foothills, near East River Road by 1931, that the Catalina Foothills School District was formed. Nine students attended classes in a garage. In 1939 Murphey will sell the district its first land for a school, just north of East River Road.

In the early 1930s Murphey teams up with Swiss-born architect Josias Joesler to begin development of what we would call today a master-planned community in the Catalina Foothills. Their objective is to attract wealthy easterners seeking a winter residence in the desert. Joesler designs large, luxurious southwestern and Mexican style homes for substantial lots, many with views of Tucson. Construction starts in 1935 on Catalina Foothills Estates, just northeast of the intersection of North Campbell Avenue and East River Road.

Saint Phiip's in the Hills Episcopal Church was designed by famed Catalina Foothills architect Josias Joesler and built by John Murphey in 1936. (Courtesy of Bob Ring)

117

For more than two decades Murphey and Joesler will collaborate on hundreds of buildings as Catalina Estates extends north, up the foothills – on both sides of today's North Campbell Avenue, and east along the mountains. There will eventually be ten Catalina Foothills Estates subdivisions.

Roads and Traffic

You watch as a series of bridges are built across the Rillito River and a network of roads is completed in the foothills, enabling further housing development. In the mid-1930s, you see North Sabino Canyon Road completed to provide access to the Sabino Canyon Recreation Area. By 1940 East River Road will extend along the Rillito River and Tanque Verde Wash all the way to North Sabino Canyon Road. Also by 1940 North Campbell Avenue will reach northward into the foothills. You will see North Hacienda del Sol Road and North Pontatoc Road by 1950, North Swan Road by 1960, and North First Avenue and North Craycroft Road by 1965. East Ina Road will extend along the mountains from the west almost to North Campbell Avenue by 1955 and further east via East Skyline Drive to North Swan Road by 1965. East Sunrise Drive will be completed across the northeastern foothills to North Sabino Canyon Road by 1975.

A side benefit of the road network's expanding northward will be access to hiking trails in the National Forest. By 1975 there will be a detailed guide available for the popular routes and trails in the Santa Catalina Mountains.

Traffic in the Catalina Foothills will increase rapidly. Over the years you will see road improvement programs, like the widening of North Swan Road that will cause dissension from opponents who will derisively call them "freeway" projects. The idea of a cross-town freeway through the Catalina Foothills will come up again and again, but will be beat back by proponents of "protecting" the foothills from such "trashy" development.

You understand that the Catalina Foothills are outside Tucson city limits, in Pima County, and how that affects taxes and services provided.

The possibility of a bridge over Sabino Creek on Snyder Road to connect the foothills area immediately south of Sabino Canyon with the Bear Canyon area to the east will also be a controversial issue. Proponents will argue that the Snyder Bridge is needed to reduce traffic congestion on East Tanque Verde Road and improve emergency vehicle response. Naysayers will counter that the bridge would bring heavy, noisy traffic to the area and degrade an important riparian environment along Sabino Creek. You will observe a spirited debate among foothills residents in 2005, trying to influence the Regional Transportation Authority Plan for road improvement. Voters will defeat the Snyder Bridge idea in a special election.

Development Expands!

Residential expansion will generally be towards the east. By 2009 the Catalina Foothills will have more than 20 gated communities such as Skyline Country Club Estates, starting in the early 1960s. The private Skyline Country Club, together with a golf course, will open in 1963. Rancho Sin Vacas will start development in the late 1970s, La Paloma Estates and Ventana Canyon Estates in the 1980s, Cobblestone in the 1990s, and Sabino Mountain and Pima Canyon in the 2000s. Several large non-gated subdivisions will also appear, including Alta Vista, Cimarron Estates, and Fairfield - starting in the 1970s and 1980s.

Apartments, town homes, and patio homes will also be built in addition to single-family homes. Not all of these developments will be greeted with happiness by long-time residents.

Other developments will support the increasing number of residents. Catalina Foothills High School will open in 1992. Retirement and nursing facilities will be built to serve the older population - Santa Catalina Villas in 1988 and Freedom Inn at Ventana Canyon in 1998. Two recreational parks will open on East River Road - George Mehl Foothills District Park in

1989, opposite North Pontatoc Road, and Brandi Fenton Memorial Park near North Dodge Blvd in 2005. La Paloma Urgent Care and Physicians Offices will start operating on East Sunrise Drive in late 2008.

Landmarks

Four Foothills landmarks will catch your attention: the familiar three radio transmission towers constructed just off North Swan Road (the dirt road extension, before paving) in 1951; the DeGrazia Gallery in the Sun built in 1965 on North Swan Road, north of East Sunrise Drive; the dramatic Rancho Sin Vacas entry portico, the former entrance arch from the El Conquistador Hotel on East Broadway Blvd, where the El Con shopping center sits now; and Anthony's in the Catalinas restaurant that will open in 1989 on the northeast corner of East Skyline Drive and North Campbell Avenue.

The entry portico at Rancho Sin Vacas came from the old El Conquistador Hotel torn down in 1968. (Courtesy of Bob Ring)

Businesses Too!

Commercial development in the Catalina Foothills will parallel residential development. By 2009 businesses will populate all but the northeast corner of the intersection of East River Road and North Campbell Avenue. On the northeast corner will still reside Saint Philip's in the Hills Episcopal Church, designed by Josias Joesler. Shopping centers too will populate the Catalina Foothills - at East Sunrise Drive and North Swan Road, at East Sunrise Drive and North Kolb Road, and at East River Road and North Craycroft Road. The Dusenberry-River Branch Library will open at East River Road and North Craycroft Road in 1991. The largest Foothills shopping center, La Encantada, at East Skyline Drive and North Campbell Avenue, where you started your time travel journey, will open in 2004.

Are We Done Yet?

The Catalina Foothills' population grows rapidly. In 1997 you will see voters reject an attempt to incorporate the area as a separate city. The 2000 census will count over 51,000 residents in ZIP codes 85718 and 85750. By 2009 development is dense; little land is left for future building. In fact you will see new housing start to creep higher onto the steeper slopes of the mountain foothills, at the edge of the Coronado National Forest, and you will wonder if this practice will continue unabated.

Housing is beginning to encroach in the upper foothills of the Santa Catalina Mountains. (Courtesy of Bob Ring

Development of the Tanque Verde Valley

(Time-machine clock: 1935)

Northeast Tucson

While you watched the start of development in the Catalina Foothills, there is similar activity beginning in Northeast Tucson. Concurrent with the government-funded efforts in Sabino Canyon and on the Catalina Highway to Mount Lemmon, you note in the mid-1930s that East Speedway Blvd extends to North Wilmot Road, which intersects with East Tanque Verde Road to provide access to the Tanque Verde Valley. Tucson city limits gradually move eastward. East Grant Road will extend to East Tanque Verde Road by 1960.

In 1948 you will see Tucson Country Club built, with accompanying golf course, just south of Tanque Verde Creek, northwest of today's East Tanque Verde Road and North Sabino Canyon Road intersection. By the mid-1950s you will see construction start on Tucson Country Club Estates, situated around the golf course, and nearby Indian Ridge Estates.

Commercial development on East Tanque Verde Road keeps pace with residential development. A little to the west of the intersection of East Tanque Verde Road and East Grant Road, you will note the building of the Trail Dust Town movie set in 1963 and further west you will see the start of "Restaurant Row," with the opening of Cork'n Cleaver (now Jonathan's Cork) in 1969. This is just the beginning; by 2009 East Tanque Verde Road will be "wall-to-wall" businesses from North Wilmot Road to North Sabino Canyon Road.

Dorado Country Club and golf course will be built in 1970, situated north of East Speedway Blvd, south of the intersection of today's East Tanque Verde Road and North Kolb Road. Housing construction around the golf course will start immediately thereafter. By 2009 commercial development will "fill in" among subdivisions, townhomes, and apartments on East Speedway Blvd from North Wilmot Road to North Kolb Road.

Access to the Valley

In parallel with this "progress," you see roads being extended to the east, and a network of north-south roads connecting them that will enable development of the Tanque Verde Valley.

In the mid-1930s you note that East Tanque Verde Road extends as a dirt road from the East Catalina Highway turnoff to near the start of the Coronado National Forest where it becomes East Redington Road. By the 1950s and 1960s East Tanque Verde Road and East Speedway Blvd will be completed to the boundary of the Coronado National Forest.

By the mid-1960s East Wrightstown Road, North Pantano Road, and North Camino Seco will be constructed - between East Tanque Verde Road and East Speedway Blvd. In the late 1960s North Houghton and North Harrison Roads will be opened south of East Tanque Verde Road.

North of East Tanque Verde Road, you will notice that North Bear Canyon Road is completed in the 1940s. East Snyder Road will be constructed in the mid-1960s, along with North Melpomene Way and North Soldier Trail, with extensions of North Houghton and North Harrison Roads coming along in the mid-1970s.

Because of these new roads, residential development in the Tanque Verde Valley explodes in the 1960s and 1970s. Land is plentiful. Some people want room to keep horses. Sprawling ranch style homes are in vogue. There is room to build your own house that is not part of a large subdivision. There is also room for golf courses and parks.

Central Valley

Development starts to the north of East Tanque Verde Road and west of East Catalina Highway, with North Bear Canyon, North Harrison, and East Snyder Roads opening the area for homes. Canyon Heights, Tres Lomas and other subdivisions will start construction in the 1970s. By 1972 you will see Sabino High School built to support the rapidly increasing population. Just north of Sabino High School, nestled up against the Santa Catalina Mountains, the Raven Golf Club will be built in 1996. Sabino Springs gated community of fine homes will be constructed around the golf course starting in the late 1990s. In 2002 Raven Golf Club will be sold and emerge as today's world-class Arizona National Golf Club.

McDonald District Park will open in the early 1980s and will offer off-leash dog areas by 2004. Kirk-Bear Canyon Branch Library will open in 1991.

Commercial development will also be booming; by 2009 shopping centers and other businesses will populate the four-corner intersections on East Tanque Verde Road, at North Bear Canyon Road and East Catalina Highway.

At the same time, you watch housing development proceed south of East Tanque Verde Road and east of North Kolb Road, with East Speedway Blvd, East Wrightstown Road, North Pantano Road, and North Camino Seco providing access to the area. In the 1970s you will see subdivision starts that include Hidden Hills Estates, Cochise Estates, Silver Shadows Estates, and Woodland Hills. The 1980s will see such subdivisions as Rosewood Estates and Wrightstown Square, plus Pantano Townhouses. The growing population will enjoy Morris K. Udall Park starting in 1982. The gated community, Lakes at Castle Rock, will be started in the late 1980s.

By 2009 businesses, townhomes, and apartments will almost completely line East Speedway Blvd from North Kolb Road to North Harrison Road. Also by 2009 East Tanque Verde Blvd, from North Kolb Road to North Pantano Road, will be almost completely commercialized, and the intersection of East Wrightstown Road and North Pantano Road will have business developments on all four corners.

Way Out East

The far eastern reaches of the Tanque Verde Valley are also being developed. In 1946 Jane Wentworth will sell her homestead that abuts Saguaro National Monument East and in 1948 residential development of the "notch" will start on 3.3-acre lots. In 1961 you'll see the Forty Niner Golf & Country Club built just northeast of the "notch," three miles east of North Houghton Road on East Tanque Verde Road. Residential housing construction will start there immediately after the Club is built. In the 1970s and 1980s you will see luxury housing starts on large view lots in places like La Cebadilla Estates and Redington Ranch, "way out east" on East Tanque Verde Road. In 1998 the Lew Sorensen Community Center, remodeled from Tanque Verde Elementary School, will open on East Tanque Verde Road, about a mile east of North Houghton Road. Meanwhile, Tanque Verde Ranch will continue to draw visitors.

Some of the later development occurs to the east of East Catalina Highway. Housing developments in this area of the Tanque Verde Valley will include Miligrosa Hills luxury homes that will start construction in the 1990s. In 1984 local businessman Roy Drachman will donate $200,000 towards the purchase of Agua Caliente Ranch; the Roy P. Drachman-Agua Caliente Regional Park will open in 1985. You will see Tanque Verde High School completed in 2005.

Agua Caliente Ranch became a park in 1985 after Tucson businessman Roy P. Drachman donated over $200,000 towards purchase of the land. (Courtesy of Bob Ring)

By the year 2000 the census will count almost 16,000 residents in ZIP code 85715 and over 18,000 people in ZIP code 85749. Nine years later in 2009 there will still be plenty of land left for development in the eastern part of the Valley.

End of Your Journey

You're almost back to the present time on your return trip from twelve million years ago. You feel your time machine gear down. Oops, you overshoot a little. It's the year 2050! You look over the Catalina Foothills and Tanque Verde Valley. Gosh! Would you ever have thought … ?

Chapter 7

Historic Critical Resources

For thousands of years, Tucsonans have depended on the critical resources of its surrounding mountains and life-giving water.

Mountain Riches

I've looked at the mountains around Tucson for years in wonderment and awe, appreciating their beauty, but lately realized that I had some questions. How many mountain ranges are there? Where did they come from? What ... ? Anyway, I put this little "primer" together to answer some of those questions; perhaps you'd be interested too.

Tucson at 2,643 feet elevation is surrounded by six mountain ranges - all within 40 miles of downtown - with the highest peaks approaching 9,500 feet.

The story begins tens of millions of years ago with a period of intense folding and faulting of the earth's crust. That was followed by slow stretching during which the crust broke up into huge blocks along the faults. Some blocks dropped, forming basins or valleys, while adjacent areas rose, forming mountain ranges. The result of this "basin and range" geologic activity, plus millions of years of erosion from wind, rain, and streams, is the miracle of Tucson's mountains.

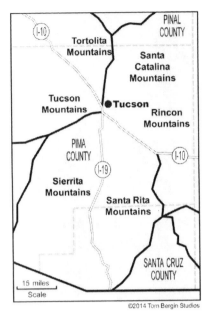

There are six mountain ranges within 40 miles of downtown Tucson. (Courtesy of Tom Bergin)

The **Santa Catalina Mountains**, just north of the city, are the largest and most complex of the mountain ranges surrounding Tucson. There are more than 50 separate peaks, over half not even named. Since 1908 the Catalinas have been designated as part of the Coronado National Forest. The Catalinas are the source of Sabino Creek that drains into the Rillito River and Cañada del Oro Creek that drains into the Santa Cruz River.

It is said that in the 1690s Italian-born missionary Eusebio Kino named the mountains after his sister's patron saint, Catarina (Catherine of Sienna, 1347-1380). It wasn't until the 1890s that the Spanish form of Catherine, "Catalinas," permanently replaced the Italian form in maps and documents.

From the 1860s to the 1960s the Catalinas' history included sporadic and largely unsuccessful gold, silver, and copper mining.

The Catalinas are Tucson's most popular place for mountain recreation, including hiking, biking, climbing, camping, and picnicking. Favorite sites include Sabino Canyon and Bear Canyon on the range's east side and Catalina State Park in the western foothills.

Most of us have driven up the beautiful "Sunrise Highway" from Tanque Verde Blvd to the charming village of Summerhaven near the Catalinas' highest peak, Mount Lemmon at 9,157 feet elevation. Mount Lemmon Ski Valley is the southernmost ski destination in the United States.

Tucson residents appreciate the beauty of the Santa Catalina Mountains, shown here covered in snow. (Courtesy of Bob Ring)

In 2003 the month-long Aspen fire seared almost 85,000 acres of land and destroyed 340 homes and businesses in Summerhaven. Since then the village has been slowly rebuilding and Tucsonans are rediscovering the Catalinas.

Miners are also rediscovering the Catalina's with the Oracle Ridge underground copper mine due to reopen soon on the back side of the mountains.

To the east of Tucson, separated from the Santa Catalina's by Reddington Pass, are the **Rincon Mountains**. The Spanish word "rincon" means "corner," the basic top-down footprint of the mountain range.

The Rincons are made up of a few broad peaks rather then a large number of jagged peaks. In fact, when you're driving east on Speedway Blvd it's hard to believe that you're looking at a substantial range of mountains. But Mica Mountain at 8,664 feet and Rincon Peak at 8,482 feet are certainly worthy mountains. Tanque Verde and Agua Caliente Creeks flow out of the Rincons, before draining into the Rillito River. Like the Catalinas, the Rincons are part of the Coronado National Forest.

Most of the Rincon Mountains are contained within Saguaro National Park East, or in the surrounding Rincon Mountain Wilderness.

The Rincon Mountain Wilderness has no major access road. The majority of the Wilderness is off-limits to motor vehicles and bicycles, but can be accessed by horseback or on foot for day-hiking or back packing from surrounding forest routes and trails.

The **Santa Rita Mountains**, also part of the Coronado National Forest, lie some 25-40 miles southeast of Tucson. The mountains are named for the patron saint of impossible causes, Saint Rita of Cascia (1381-1457). Some of the earliest silver mining in Arizona occurred in the Santa Ritas, beginning in the 1850s. The highest peak in the range, and the highest point in the Tucson area, is Mount Wrightson at 9,453 feet.

There is no road to the top of Mount Wrightson, but there is a paved road from I-19 into the northwestern part of the Santa Ritas to Madera Canyon, one of the world's premier birding areas and a favorite of Tucsonans for picnicking, hiking and camping.

The Smithsonian Institution's Fred Whipple Observatory sits atop nearby Mount Hopkins at 8,560 feet.

In July 2005 the massive Florida fire burned over 23,000 acres, mostly in wilderness areas.

Currently the Santa Rita Mountains are involved in a controversy over copper mining. The proposed open-pit Rosemont Mine would occupy 4,500 acres of the Rosemont Ranch on the north flank of the mountain range. Opponents raise both economic and environmental issues.

Roughly 30 miles southwest of Tucson, just west of Green Valley and Sahuarita, lie the **Sierrita Mountains,** almost totally ignored in any listing of Tucson-area mountain ranges. Living up to the meaning of their name, "little mountains," the Sierritas offer mid-elevation, somewhat scrubby peaks and lower, gentle hills, cut deeply by valleys. The range has been a popular site for cattle ranching and mining explorations since 1900. Keystone Peak tops the local mountains at 6,188 feet.

The attraction for visitors is pleasant solitude, a rich dose of mining history, and a "non-park" experience. Much of the land lies on private property and access to parts of the Sierritas, for example the Keystone Peak Trail, may have to be negotiated.

Mining continues today on the northeastern side of the Sierritas in two enormous open-pit copper mines: Freeport McMoRan's Sierrita Mine and ASARCO's Mission Mine.

The open pit of the Mission Mine is 2 miles long by 2 miles wide and is 1500 feet deep. The copper mine operates 24 hours a day, 365 days a year. (Courtesy of ASARCO)

The familiar **Tucson Mountains,** just west of Tucson, are named for the city they frame with beautiful Arizona sunsets. The relatively low summits, with Wasson Peak the highest at 4,687 feet, "do not escape the desert."

Tucson Mountain Park, established in 1929, protects the natural resource area that includes rock art, Hohokam ruins, and old mines. The Park provides non-motorized shared-use trails for hikers, equestrians, and mountain bikers with access from several paved roads, particularly Gates Pass Road, along the old 1880s stagecoach route from Tucson to Quijotoa. Picnicking and wildlife viewing opportunities are located throughout the park.

Additional recreation areas located with the Tucson Mountains include Saguaro National Park West, the renowned Arizona-Sonora Desert Museum, and Old Town Studios. And, since 2005 the Tucson Mountains have been the home of JW Marriott Starr Pass Resort & Spa.

Perhaps the most recognizable of Tucson Mountain sites is Sentinel Peak at 2,887 feet, formerly a lookout point for the Spanish on the western edge of Tucson. In 1915 fans of the University of Arizona football team whitewashed a large "A" on its side to celebrate a victory. The tradition continues today on "A" Mountain with the permanent red, white, and blue "A."

The lowest of Tucson's surrounding mountain ranges are the **Tortolita Mountains**, on Tucson's northwest, on the northern boundaries of Marana and Oro Valley. The Tortilitas nevertheless feature rugged peaks, gullies and canyons, vast strands of cacti, and a rich ranching history. The unnamed highest peak in the Tortilitas rises to 4,652 feet.

The Tortolitas (little turtle doves) were named for the multitudes of small doves that were present in the area until the early 1900s.

Much of the mountain range is protected by Tortilita Mountain Park, established in 1986 at 3,000 acres and steadily expanding since. Southeast of Tortilita Mountain Park lies Honeybee Village, a former Hohokam pueblo, and nearby is Honeybee Canyon, a riparian area with one of Pima County's only perennial streams, Honeybee Creek. Both areas offer hiking and picnicking.

Beginning in the 1990s there has been considerable conflict between environmentalists and the developers of resorts, golf courses, and million dollar homes in the southern foothills of the Tortilitas. Access to Tortilita Mountain Park, especially from Marana, has also become contentious.

Remember, that's **six** mountain ranges within a one-hour drive of downtown Tucson! How many have you visited?

Life-Giving Water

For the last three thousand years, Tucson's waterways (rivers, streams, creeks, etc.) ran freely much of the time and were a reliable source of water for everyday use and for irrigation farming. The beneficiaries of this plentiful water included the predecessors of the Hohokam, the Hohokam and their descendants, early Spanish, Mexican and American settlers, and finally Tucson residents. But, in the last 100 years, that reliable water source has disappeared, leaving mostly dry streambeds. What happened and how was Tucson's water resource renewed?

Waterways

The Santa Cruz River and the waterways that drain into it were the primary source of water for Tucson. Those waterways included Sabino Creek, out of the Santa Catalina Mountains; Agua Caliente Creek and Tanque Verde Creek, out of the Rincons; and Pantano Creek, fed from Agua Verde and Rincon Creeks, southeast of Tucson - all flowed into the Rillito River which in turn drained into the Santa Cruz River. Cañada del Oro Creek, out of the Santa Catalinas, drained directly into the Santa Cruz River.

According to the book, *Arizona's Changing Rivers: How People Have Affected the Rivers*, the Santa Cruz River once was active all year round from it headwaters in the San Rafael Valley, southeast of Patagonia, south to Mexico, and then turning north to about Tubac, often as a series of marshes (cienegas), rather than a flowing river.

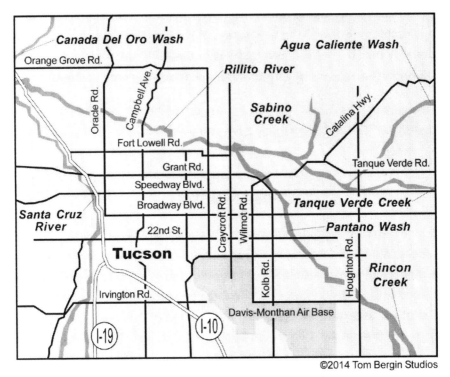

©2014 Tom Bergin Studios

There are six principal waterways in the Tucson area. (Courtesy of Tom Bergin)

From Tubac the river went underground, surfaced near San Xavier del Bac mission, and from there alternated between above ground and underground until surfacing at a dependable water hole at the north end of the Tucson Mountains. To the north, the river apparently "ended in the desert" prior to reaching the Gila River, except during floods. Springs between San Xavier and the Rillito River created marshes and added to the flow just west of Tucson.

In 1881, with Tucson's population around 7,000 people, the Tucson Water Company began delivering piped water from the Santa Cruz River into town. Until 1887, Tucson residents could purchase river water for a penny a gallon from vendors who transported it in bags draped over burros' backs. After that, water was sold by the bucket or barrel and delivered door-to-door in wagons.

The decline of the Santa Cruz River as a water source for Tucson began in 1887. Samuel Hughes (prominent in the incorporation of the City of Tucson and establishment of public education) attempted to increase the water supply to his fields north of St. Mary's Road. Interfering with an existing network of irrigation canals, he built a new, deep ditch to tap the subsurface flow of the river.

Large floods during the next four years caused this ditch and others to rapidly erode - both downward and laterally. Gravity irrigation with surface water was no longer possible. However, by using wells to draw water from underground river flow and cement-lined canals, agriculture continued in the Tucson urban area.

During this same period irrigation farming was also being conducted along the Rillito River at places like the Mormon settlement of Binghampton and at Old Fort Lowell.

Groundwater

Thankfully, there was another source of water besides rivers to provide for Tucson's growing needs - underground water. Beneath the Tucson Valley, formed in the same Basin and Range geological events that created Tucson's mountain ranges and the subsequent erosion from those mountains, lies a tremendous mass of porous sediments filled with water deposited during long ago glacial periods and over thousands of years, from seepage of rain and snowmelt runoff. This body of water-filled sediments (aquifer) extends from very near the surface of the Tucson Valley in some places, down to 1,200 feet deep - and in the 1890s probably contained an incredible 20-"plus" cubic miles of water.

Tucson began pumping that groundwater in the 1890s when the Tucson Water Company constructed 20-foot deep wells all over the Tucson metropolitan area. As more and more water was pumped out of the ground, the underground flow of the Santa Cruz and Rillito Rivers essentially "dried up," bringing an end to irrigation farming along the rivers by the 1930s.

In 1940, with Tucson's population at nearly 37,000 people, Tucson began increasing its groundwater pumping and for decades, groundwater was our only water source. We pumped groundwater faster than nature could replace it (natural recharge from rain and snow melt), causing the water table in some places to drop more than 200 feet. Groundwater pumping also caused the land in some places to sink and drew off water from riparian areas.

By 1970 Tucson's population had exploded to more than 260,000 people. Unless we wanted to mine underground water down to the last drop, something else had to be done!

Central Arizona Project

That "something else" was truly amazing! In 1938 Parker Dam was completed as one of a series of dams to help control and regulate the once unruly Colorado River. Parker Dam's primary purpose was to provide reservoir storage for water to be diverted to the states of California, Arizona, Nevada, Utah, Colorado, Wyoming, New Mexico and to Mexico.

For four decades lawmakers argued about how to allocate Colorado River water among its claimants, how to manage this critical resource, and the priorities for use of the water in the various states. Arizona got its act together in the late 1960s and early 1970s with, as the *Arizona Republic* reported, "probably the state's most celebrated bipartisan achievement of the 20th century," which led to the approval of the Central Arizona Project (CAP) to divert water from

This 336-mile canal of the Central Arizona Project brings water to Tucson from the Colorado River. (Courtesy of Wikimedia Commons)

the Colorado River from Lake Havasu City into central and southern Arizona.

Construction of the project, the largest and most expensive aqueduct system ever built in the United States, began in 1973. Over a period of 20 years, workers built a 336-mile diversion canal, from the Colorado River to just southwest of Tucson, and in 1992 officials "turned on the faucet" to start providing Tucson with water to supplement our limited groundwater.

In 2001, after resolving some CAP water-quality problems, Tucson began blending CAP water and underground water before delivering it to users.

Today and the Future

Today, with the population of Tucson exceeding 520,000 and growing steadily, we are operating under the Tucson Water Department's Long Range Water Plan 2000-2050.

We have stopped pumping most of the wells where the water table has dropped significantly and where the loss of riparian areas and sinking of the land has been most damaging. As a result, the water table has begun to rise slightly in some areas. The goal is to "limit our pumping to no more than the rate of natural replenishment [so] we can still use this resource without causing environmental damage."

In an effort to conserve water, Tucson is recharging groundwater supplies by running some of the CAP water into local rivers to seep into the aquifer.

Tucson is also using increasing amounts of reclaimed water (treated wastewater) for irrigation, dust control, and industrial uses.

As we look ahead to meeting future water demands, we are naturally concerned about possible significant effects of climate change and prolonged draughts. In a front page story in the *Arizona Daily Star* on July 29, 2012, Tony Davis, wrote about how southern Arizona streams are drying up. Riparian and recreation areas are suffering! Even the mighty

Colorado River, the source of our CAP water, is reporting near record lows.

So Tucson faces real water challenges for the future. Can we conserve enough water to make a difference? Could we transport groundwater from less populated areas into Tucson? Could we cover the CAP canal to prevent water losses from evaporation - perhaps with solar panels as some have suggested? Are artificial snowmaking and cloud seeding applicable to increase fresh water runoff to the Colorado River? Could we desalinate deep-aquifer brackish groundwater or ocean water?

The answers to these questions may determine the future of Tucson.

Chapter 8

Historical Odds and Ends

The following three stories spotlight the unique histories of three Tucson buildings.

Hotel Congress Fire and the Capture of John Dillinger

For ten months in 1933, John Dillinger and his gang terrorized the Midwest with multiple bank robberies, wild chases, daring prison breaks, and violent machine gun battles.

In January, 1934 Dillinger and three of his gang were "laying low" in Tucson, two gang members at the Congress Hotel, while the police and FBI were madly searching back east for "Public Enemy No. 1."

The three-story Congress Hotel was built in 1919 - the same year that the nation's first municipally owned airport opened in Tucson. On the morning of January 23, 2014 a fire broke out in the basement of the hotel. The first alert was by telephone at 7:16 am as recorded in the Tucson Fire Department's "Daily Report of Fires." TFD history records, written after the fire, tell the story:

> "1-23-1934 Congress Hotel … 3rd fire in month. 15 yr. old bldg. valued at $250,000. Day clerk Mrs. Helga Nelson stayed at telephone exchange box awakening guests.

Went dead as she finished calling 2nd floor guests. P.D. [Police Department] and employees ran thru 3rd floor to warn guests. Started near oil furnace and oil supply. 3 general alarms brought every piece of equipment. Roberts = chief. [2 ladder trucks] 5 pumpers. ... Flames spread up elevator shaft. 100 guests got out safely. ... Roof fell in at 8 a.m. Cupola over front entrance fell at 8:30 ... extinguished by 10:30 a.m. ... 3rd floor wrecked, rest of building flooded."

Firemen helped hotel guests escape from the third floor of the hotel with a ladder. A couple of distraught men offered two firemen a $12 tip to go back up the ladder and retrieve their luggage. The firefighters remembered that several pieces of the luggage were very heavy.

Firefighters stream water into the third floor of the Congress Hotel during the fire on January 23, 1934. (Courtesy of Tommy Stefanski)

Later, back at the fire station, while reading *True Detective* magazine, the firemen recognized the two men from the fire as Dillinger gang members and wanted fugitives. They reported the luggage incident to the police who began a surveillance operation at the address where the heavy luggage was delivered after the fire.

On January 25th John Dillinger and his three gang members were arrested without incident at three different locations in downtown Tucson. The heavy luggage was found to contain machine guns, rifles, pistols, revolvers, and bullet proof vests - far more firepower than Tucson police officers had.

Dillinger was extradited to Chicago where a month later he escaped jail using a fake carved pistol. Five months after that on July 22, 1934 Dillinger was shot dead by FBI agents while resisting arrest when exiting the Biograph Theater in Chicago.

The Congress Hotel was renovated and today offers 40 vintage rooms, a restaurant with sidewalk seating, nightclub, salon, and banquet room. The building was added to the National Historic Register in 2003.

Since 1992 Tucson has honored the capture of John Dillinger with an annual Dillinger Days celebration, stressing Tucson's role in history. Re-enactments relive the Dillinger gang's last bank robbery in Chicago prior to their arrival in Tucson, as well as the series of events leading to the gang's capture in and around Downtown.

Tucson International Airport's Huge Wooden Hangars

During World War II Davis-Monthan field was both an Army Air Base and Tucson's civilian airport. Seeing a need to separate military and civilian operations, in 1940 Tucson officials purchased land about five miles southwest of Davis-Monthan for a future Tucson municipal airport. But before the dream of a new civilian airport could be realized, another urgent requirement to support the war effort arose. The U.S. needed a place to modify and outfit long range bomber aircraft before sending them into battle. So in 1942 Consolidated Vultee Aircraft (later Convair division of General Dynamics) built three enormous hangars (and runways) at the new airport site to modify B-24 Liberator bombers.

The hangars were built out of wood because steel was scarce during the war. Each of the three hangars was approximately 750 feet long, 250 feet wide, with curved Quonset-hut-shape roofs and 40-foot high sliding steel/glass-paned doors on each end. The center area of the hangars was open from the floor to the roof structure to accommodate large aircraft, but along the sides there was a second story (mezzanine) for testing of aircraft avionics. Huge 12-foot diameter swamp coolers were placed on the roofs along the sides of the hangars, with wooden ducts to the inside to disperse cooled air. The narrow space between the hangars accommodated a cafeteria and tool cribs.

A firehouse was built about a hundred yards off the northeast corner of the hangar complex. It's still there today, but in a fenced, no-trespassing area.

Consolidated Vultee designed the B-24 aircraft and built them in their San Diego plant and several other factories around the country. Tucson was one of five sites that modified the new planes. Two types of operations were performed in Tucson as described in the July 1944 issue of *Popular Mechanics* magazine. Twenty five percent of the effort was directed at preparations to get aircraft ready for the particular climate and operating conditions of the theater the aircraft would be deployed to. Seventy five per cent of the efforts involved improvements to the aircrafts' offense and defense systems.

Following World War II in 1947 the Tucson Municipal Airport moved from Davis-Monthan field to the new location. Then in 1948 the Tucson Airport Authority was formed as a nonprofit organization whose mission was "development and promotion of transportation and commerce by air; operation and maintenance of airfields in Southern Arizona; and advocacy and support of all projects, activities and legislation for the benefit of commerce by air."

Tucson Municipal Airport operated on the west side of the airfield, alongside the three hangars that were oriented roughly north-south. The airline passenger terminal occupied spaces towards the north end of the east side of the eastern-most of the three hangars (Hangar 1). This hangar-side terminal remained in operation for 15 years until 1963 when the terminal moved to its current location and the airport earned the designation of Tucson International Airport.

Tucson's hangar-side passenger terminal with an American Airlines DC-7 shown on the apron off the covered gate ramp. Aerial view, looking west, around 1960. (Courtesy of Tucson Airport Authority)

Meanwhile aircraft modification work had continued in the three hangars. In 1950, preparing for the Korean War, the Grand Central Aircraft Company leased the hangars to restore and modify B-29 bombers that had been mothballed at Davis-Monthan AFB since the end of World War II. Grand Central also modified new jet-powered B-47 bombers for the Boeing Company. The Grand Central Service in Tucson (along with another facility in Glendale, California) was recognized as the largest repair, overhaul, and modification station in the country.

Grand Central Aircraft Company modified U.S. Air Force B-29 bombers in the three hangars from 1948-1952. Aerial view, looking south, around 1950. (Courtesy of Tucson Airport Authority)

From the mid-1950s to 1958 McDonnell Douglas Corporation used the hangars to overhaul civilian aircraft like the DC-6 and DC-7.

In 1969 the newly approved Pima College (later Pima Community College) used the mezzanine of one of the hangars as a temporary campus. Today, the Aviation Technology branch of Pima Community College is located in a modern building just a few hundred yards south of the hangars.

Under the auspices of the Tucson Airport Authority the hangars began a transition from supporting aircraft modifications to warehousing aviation parts and equipment. Today five aviation companies lease space in the hangars to store parts, mostly filling the available (442,000 square feet) of space.

Tucson's version of "Rosie the Riveter." Women at B-29 modification stations inside a hangar, around 1950. (Courtesy of Tucson Airport Authority)

This is what the three hangars look like today. Note the huge sliding doors. View from hangars' southeast corner. (Courtesy of Bob Ring)

Architectural Oddity: The Beau Brummel Club

Did you ever wonder about that odd-shaped building - the one that looks like an old drive-in food establishment - near the northeast corner of N. Main Avenue and W. Speedway Boulevard? In fact, the building opened as Dukes Drive-In in the early 1940s, offering eating from your car or inside at a counter and booths. Today, the building is the home of the Beau Brummel Club, a private social organization.

The Beau Brummel Club was established in 1936 by small group of African American men "who were refused entrance into Anglo social clubs of that era." The founders included Colonel Reuben L. Horner III, one of the most decorated blacks of World War II, and Duke Shaw, who would later build and operate Dukes Drive-In.

The Club was named after the iconic Beau Brummell who lived in England in the early 1800s and is famous for introducing modern men's fashions, like the suit worn with a tie. For an unknown reason, the Club's name "dropped" the second "l" in Brummell.

Initially the group was limited to 15 men, supported education and social services in the African American community, and provided a sort of hospitality welcome for blacks new to Tucson. Club members started out meeting in each other's houses, held a popular annual formal dance at the old Blue Moon ballroom (burned down in 1947), brought in entertainment like Louis Armstrong, and held picnics on Mount Lemmon and in Sabino Canyon.

The Beau Brummel Club was also helpful in the integration of major league baseball. In 1947, starting a 15-year relationship with our town, Bill Veeck, owner of the Cleveland Indians, brought his newly integrated team to Tucson for spring training. The Pioneer Hotel, the team headquarters, had a strict "whites only" policy then so Dukes Drive-In became the place for black professional baseball players to eat and socialize. This included such Cleveland Indians stars as Larry Doby, Satchel Paige, and Harry "Suitcase" Simpson.

At first Beau Brummel members hosted black Cleveland Indians in their homes. But Duke Shaw built a ten-unit motel just to the south of the Club to accommodate the baseball players and visiting black entertainers

In 1954 the drive-in was expanded and the Beau Brummel Club moved into a portion of the building with, as current member and local attorney Rubin Salter says, "great fanfare." The Beau Brummel Club took over the whole building when the drive-in restaurant was shut down in the 1970s. The motel lasted until 2005 when it was torn down, after being abandoned for several years.

The Beau Brummel Club is still active today. The Club has changed its all-male, blacks-only policy and now is more racially diverse and includes women. According to attorney Salter, the membership is mostly professional, including people from IBM and Raytheon for instance. Currently the Club has 20 members on the Corporate Board, but sells "access cards" for $10 to an average of a hundred people a year.

The Club is primarily for members, who enjoy getting together to play cards or dominoes; younger members are attracted more to sports-related activities. Both members and those with access cards make use of the full-service bar in the Club.

Occasionally the Club sponsors musical events, hosting visiting bands with an emphasis on "Downhome Blues," according to Rubin Salter's son, Kristian, also an attorney.

The Club has maintained its community service mission by holding tailgate parties at University of Arizona football games, sponsoring an annual Ghetto Open golfing event for charity at local courses, and hosting an annual ball for members and invited guests.

The Beau Brummel Club faces two threats to its future. The first - a sign of the times - is the difficulty of maintaining successful private fraternal organizations and social clubs in an increasingly impersonal, electronic-messaging society. The second threat - to the building - is the probable future redevelopment of the entire just-north-of-town-center area.

The Beau Brummel Club building at 1148 N. Main Avenue has a storied history. (Courtesy of Bob Ring)

But, since 1936 the Beau Brummel Club has survived, thrived, and become a worthwhile community institution. As the Club's namesake Englishman Beau Brummell might say, "Good show and good luck for the future!"

Primary Sources

1. American Jewish Historical Society.
2. *Another Tucson* (Bonnie Henry, 1992).
3. *Arizona: A Cavalcade of History* (Marshall Trimble, 1989).
4. *Arizona: A Celebration of the Grand Canyon State* (Jim Turner, 2011).
5. *Arizona: A History* (Thomas E. Sheridan, 2012).
6. "Arizona History Makers," Arizona Historical Society, 2010.
7. "Arizona Jewish Pioneers," Southwest Jewish Archives.
8. *Arizona Place Names* (Byrd H. Granger, 1985).
9. *Arizona, A Short History* (Odie B. Faulk, 1970).
10. *Arizona's Changing Rivers: How People Have Changed the Rivers* (Tellman, et. al., 1997).
11. *Arizona Territory Post Offices & Postmasters* (John and Lillian Theobald, 1961).
12. "Beau Brummel Club Tucson," Tumblr.com.
13. Binghampton Newspaper Articles: *Arizona Daily Star* (September 15, 1991); *Tucson Citizen* (February 28, 2005); *Desert Leaf* (January 2008).
14. Brandi Fenton Park.
15. "Frank Busch Biography," the University of Arizona Official Athletic Site.
16. *Butterfield Overland Mail, 1857-1869* (Roscoe Conkling, 1947).
17. "Butterfield Overland Mail Company Stagecoaches and Stage (Celerity) Wagons used on the Southern Trail, 1859-1861," (Gerald T. Ahnert, 2013).
18. "Butterfield Overland National Historic Trail Special Resource Study / Environmental Assessment," *Trail Study News*, January 2012.

19. "Butterfield Overland Trail," Frank Norris, *Desert Tracks*, January, 2015.

20. *The Butterfield Trail and Overland Mail Company in Arizona, 1858-1861* (Gerald T. Ahnert, 2011).

21. "The Butterfield Trail Revisited," *The Smoke Signal* (Stan Brown, 2007).

22. "Mike Candrea Biography," the University of Arizona Official Athletic Site.

23. "Cienega Creek, other S. AZ. Streams, increasingly dry," *Arizona Daily Star* (Tony Davis, July 29, 2012).

24. "Crypto-Jews," New Mexico Jewish Historical Society.

25. "Cultural History of the Tucson Basin," *Desert Archaeology Tucson* (J. Homer Thiel and Michael W. Diehl, 2004).

26. "Cultural Resources Assessment for the Fort Lowell Park … ," (J. Homer Thiel, 2009).

27. "Ted DeGrazia Biography," degrazia-art.com.

28. Dillinger Days website.

29. *Encyclopedia of Stagecoach Robbery in Arizona* (R. Michael Wilson, 2003).

30. FBI website - Famous Cases and Criminals.

31. "Fort Lowell Historic District: Portfolio II," Arizona Historical Society, 2004.

32. Fort Lowell Park Master Plan (2009).

33. *Frontier Lady of Letters: The Heroic Love Story of Ines Fraser* (Bob Ring, et. al., 2007).

34. *Isabella Greenway – An Enterprising Woman* (Kristie Miller, 2005).

35. "Greenway, John Campbell and Isabella," Arizona Historical Society, MS0311.

36. "Emil Walter Haury, Biographical Memoirs," National Academy of Sciences.

37. *Historical Atlas of Arizona* (Henry Walker and Don Bufkin, 1979).

38. "Historical Facts of Tucson's African American Community," tucsonalumnae.org.

39. "History of Binghampton Ward," Edna Bingham Sabin, leongoodman.tripod.com.

40. *A History of the Jews in New Mexico* (Henry J. Tobias, 1990).
41. "A History of the Old Fort Lowell Neighborhood Association," brochure.
42. "History: The Paleo-Indians, Hispanic Culture, Spanish Missions," discoverseaz.com.
43. "Images of Binghampton: A History," ourfamiliesroots.org.
44. *The Hohokam Indians of the Tucson Basin* (Linda M. Gregonis & Karl Reinhard, 1979).
45. *The Hohokam Millennium* (Suzanne K. Fish and Paul R. Fish, 2008).
46. *Images of America*: Early Tucson (Anne I. Woosley, 2008).
47. Interview with Duane Bingham (2012).
48. Interviews with Rubin and Kristian Salter, and Effrim Griffin, (September 2012).
49. "In the Steps of Esteban: Tucson's African American Heritage," (Rueben L. Horner III, 1996).
50. *Islands in the Desert: A History of the Uplands of Southeastern Arizona* (John P. Wilson, 1995).
51. "Henry O. Jaastad: Architect of Tucson's Future," *Smoke Signal* (Mona L. McCroskey, Spring 1990).
52. Jewish Museum of the American West.
53. "Jews on the Western Frontier: An Overview," Jewish Virtual Library: Tucson (Harriet and Fred Rochlin, 1985).
54. "Josias Joesler: An Architectural Eclectic," parentseyes.arizona.edu.
55. "A Journey Back in Time - Grand Central Air Terminal," *Airport Journals*, July, 2009.
56. Long Realty Company.
57. "Man in the News: A Dedicated Heart Surgeon," *New York Times*, 1985.
58. "J. F. "Pop" McKale," Pima County Sports Hall of Fame.
59. *Mexicanos – A History of Mexicans in the United States* (Manuel G. Gonzales, 1999).
60. *Mo: The Life and Times of Morris K. Udall* (Donald W. Carson and James W. Johnson, 2004).

61. "Mormon Colonies in Mexico," Wikipedia.com.

62. *A Nice Place to Visit: A Brief History of Sabino Canyon* (Jim Turner, 2006).

63. *Occupied America – A History of Chicanos* (Rodolfo F. Acuña, 2011).

64. "Lute Olson Biography," coachluteolson.com.

65. "Overpass Memorializes Tucson's Mayor Murphy," *Arizona Daily Star* (David Leighton, September 3, 2013).

66. *Paradise Found: The Settlement of the Catalina Mountains* (Kathy Alexander, 1991).

67. *The People of Fort Lowell* (Teresa Turner, 1990).

68. "People Without Pots: Preceramic Archaeology of the Tucson Basin," *Archaeology in Tucson* (Bruce B. Huckell, PhD, 1994).

69. *Pioneer Jews: A New Life in the Far West* (Harriet and Fred Rochlin, 2000).

70. Pima County Natural Resources, Park, and Recreation Department.

71. "Regents Professor Michael J. Drake, 1946-2011," arizona.edu.

72. RE/Max Majestic Realty Company.

73. *My Reminiscences, Vol. 1* (Raphael Pumpelly, 1918).

74. "Linda Ronstadt biography," biography.com.

75. *Sabino Canyon, The Life of a Southwestern Oasis* (David Wentworth Lazaroff, 1993).

76. "San Pedro Chapel," Old Fort Lowell Neighborhood Association brochure.

77. *The Santa Catalina Mountains, A Guide to Trails and Routes* (Pete Cowgill & Eber Glendening, 1997).

78. "Seeking Freshwater for Tucson," *Desert Leaf* (Craig S. Baker, July/August 2012).

79. *Simple Dreams* (Linda Ronstadt, 2013).

80. Charles Leland (C.L.) Sonnichsen Manuscript Collection, Arizona Historical Society, 2013.

81. *Spanish Colonial Tucson* (Henry F. Dobyns, 1976).

82. "They Make Tomorrow's Planes Today," *Popular Mechanics*, July, 1944.

83. "A Thousand Years of Irrigation in Tucson," (Jonathan B. Mabry and Homer Thiel, 1995).

84. Tucson Airport Authority brochures: The History of Tucson International Airport, History of Tucson Airport Authority, Tucson Aviation History.

85. *Los Tucsonenses – The Mexican Community in Tucson, 1854-1941* (Thomas E. Sheridan, 1997).

86. Tucson Fire Department Records.

87. *Tucson: The Life and Times of an American City* (C. L. Sonnichsen, 1987).

88. "Tucson Mountain Ranges: Climbing, Hiking & Mountaineering," summitpost.org.

89. "Tucson's Pioneer Legacy: They came and existed and they farmed," Binghampton Rural Historic Landscape, *LDS Living Magazine*, January 11, 2011.

90. Tucson Territorial Pioneer Project (2008).

91. U.S. Census Data.

92. *Water for Tucson's Future: Long Range Water Plan 2000-2005.*

93. "Water Supply and Demand in Tucson," *Tucson Citizen* (Johnathan DuHamel, June 21, 2009).

94. "Andrew Weil: Arizona Center of Integrative Medicine," arizona.edu.

95. "What's happened to GOP since Goldwater," *Arizona Republic* (Dan Nowicki, January, 1, 2009).

96. "Without a Shot Fired: The 1934 Capture of the Dillinger Gang in Tucson," *The Smoke Signal*, December 2005.

97. *Wells Fargo in Arizona Territory* (John and Lillian Theobald, 1978).

98. *Zeckendorfs and Steinfelds: Merchant Princes of the American Southwest* (Bettina O'Neil Lyons, 2008).

Acknowledgements

I appreciate that the *Arizona Daily Star* provided me a forum for six years to write about the history of Tucson. And a hearty thank you to my editor, Tiffany Kjos, who constantly encouraged me and applied her considerable editing talents to my work.

Several additional individuals deserve special mention here. They include:

Gerald T. Ahnert has emerged as the country's foremost expert on the history of the Butterfield Overland Mail. He provided invaluable assistance by correcting my errors, offering suggestions of new material to include, providing critical images, and reviewing my final product.

Tom Bergin, of Tom Bergin studios here in Tucson, made most of the maps in this book.

Duane Bingham, as a direct descendant of the founders of the Rillito River Mormon community of Binghampton, helped me understand the behind the scenes story and allowed me to use rare family images.

Effrim Griffin suggested the original column on the Beau Brummel Club, helped me research the architectural history of the unique building, and set up an interview with a local attorney and current member of the Beau Brummel Club.

Bettina Lyons, author of *Zeckendorfs and Steinfelds: Merchant Princes of the American Southwest*, talked with me about early Tucson merchandizing and permitted me to include a rare historical photograph.

Viki Mathews, from the Tucson Airport Authority, enthusiastically set up a tour of the three huge wooden hangars built in 1942, arranged to have

155

historical experts on hand, and provided a number of historic images for me to include in this book.

Roger Pfeuffer, Co-Chair of Friends of Tucson, graciously set up a tour of Mission Gardens, the birthplace of Tucson, including local history experts, and then directed me to other key Tucson historians.

Al Ring, my brother and historian/archivist for the Tucson Fire Foundation, is my go-to person for Arizona historical research. He is also an avid collector of postcards depicting Arizona history, many of which are included in this book.

Patricia Stephenson, co-author of *Tom Marshall's Tucson*, a treasure house of historic Tucson photos, generously allowed me to use several images in this book.

Jim Turner, retired from the Arizona Historical Society and long-time Tucson historian, encouraged my column writing and inspired me with lectures on Tucson history.

Henry Wallace, an archaeologist at Desert Archaeology, Inc., answered my many questions about Hohokam history, reviewed my original columns, and arranged for unpublished images to be included in my story.

Pat Wood, my better half and former librarian, is my ultimate resource for library research. Moreover, she is the first and most important reviewer for all my writing.

plus ... thanks to the numerous respondents to my
newspaper columns for their kind words, corrections,
and suggested additions.

About the Author

Bob Ring is a former aerospace engineer and manager who since his retirement from Raytheon in 2000 has devoted his time to researching and writing about the history of Tucson and Arizona.

From 2003 to 2007, Bob co-wrote a bi-monthly newspaper column, "Along the Ruby Road," for the *Green Valley News & Sun*. The column highlighted the colorful history of Arizona's borderland Oro Blanco Mining District, with emphasis on the mining ghost town, Ruby.

Through 2008, Bob took part in eight Arizona History Conventions. He wrote and presented eight papers ranging from - the history of Warren, Arizona, a suburb of the famous copper mining town, Bisbee - to the mining history of the Oro Blanco district and Ruby. At the 2006 Convention, he participated in a roundtable discussion, "So You Want to Write a Book: Self-Publishing Arizona History."

Author Bob Ring.
(Courtesy of Bob Ring)

In 2005 Bob co-authored his first book, *Ruby, Arizona - Mining, Mayhem, and Murder*. This book details the century and a half history of the Montana mine and its Ruby mining camp, including two infamous double murders in the 1920s.

In 2007 Bob co-authored his second book, *Frontier Lady of Letters - The Heroic Love Story of Ines Fraser*. This personal memoir - based on letters between Ines Fraser and her beloved husband - follows Ines's inspiring story from mining in Colorado and Arizona in the early 1900s to the beginning of the manned space program in the 1960s.

In his third book, in 2008, Bob co-edited his great grandfather's memoir, *Detour to the California Gold Rush: Eugene Ring's Travels to South America, California, and Mexico, 1848-1850*. This book details the incredible tale of a young man's unplanned adventure that almost ended with his death.

From 2008-2014 Bob wrote a human interest newspaper column, "Ring's Reflections," for Tucson's *Arizona Daily Star*. Twenty nine of those columns dealt with various aspects of Tucson history, from which this book is drawn.

Bob is a Professional member of the Society of Southwest Authors.

All of Bob's projects are shared on his web site, http://ringbrothershistory.com.

CPSIA information can be obtained at www.ICGtesting.com
Printed in the USA
BVOW01s0444090315

390578BV00006B/11/P